Amphibians & Reptiles of the North Woods

Amphibians & Reptiles

of the North Woods

By Allen Blake Sheldon

Kollath+Stensaas

PUBLISHING

Kollath+Stensaas Publishing
394 Lake Avenue South, Suite 406
Duluth, MN 55802
Office: 218.727.1731
Orders: 800.678.7006
info@kollathstensaas.com
www.kollathstensaas.com

AMPHIBIANS & REPTILES
of the NORTH WOODS

Printed in Korea by Doosan Corporation
10 9 8 7 6 5 4 3 2 1   First Edition

Editorial Director: Mark Sparky Stensaas
Graphic Designer: Rick Kollath

ISBN 13: 978-0-9673793-8-8
ISBN 10: 0-9673793-8-5

Table of Contents

To Beth & Lynn,
who stopped highway traffic to save a Snapping Turtle.

Acknowledgements

First, I thank Sparky Stensaas and Rick Kollath for having the confidence to select me to write this book, especially considering the impressive quality of their previously published nature field guides

I'm grateful to my daughters, Beth and Lynn, and their mother, Kathy, for enduring occasional inconveniences, but still encouraging my interest in photographing amphibians and reptiles.

My thanks to the sharp-eyed members of the La Crosse Area Camera Club who improve my photography with 26 years of ruthless, but helpful, criticism.

This book couldn't have been researched and written without a good computer, and mine was practically non-functional, choked by a plague of viruses and other unsolicited pestilence. My generous son-in-law and computer expert, Vinay Tauro, spent many hours curing my machine, installing defenses and dispensing advice.

Many of the amphibians and reptiles pictured in this book were provided by my friends Dan Nedrelo and Bob Hay, or else found during our quests into the forests and wetlands of northern Wisconsin. They have inspired me to get out in the field more often, and we've waded through chilly marshes in the middle of the night, dragged canoes through shallow streams and flipped innumerable rocks in search of elusive critters. My thanks to other friends, including Matt Heeter, Scott Rusch and Randy Goyette, who have brought me amphibians or reptiles to photograph, directed me to locations or spotted them in the wild before I did.

Amphibians and reptiles have also been made available by the enthusiastic and knowledgeable members of the Minnesota Herpetological Society, who have brought critters to meetings and picnics or captured them during surveys.

Enjoy the book!

Allen Blake Sheldon
March 25, 2006

We at Kollath-Stensaas have been blessed with great authors; Allen continues that tradition. He met every deadline with quality work; work that sprang from his incredible knowledge of our creeping and crawling critters. Thanks Allen.

The Publishers; Mark Sparky Stensaas, Rick Kollath
April 16, 2006

Why Should I be Interested in Creepy, Crawly Critters?

Amphibians and reptiles are an integral part of the North Woods, adding to our enjoyment of nature. We might only get a glimpse as a frog leaps from shore, a turtle tumbles off a log and splashes into the water or a snake zips across a trail. But unlike most birds and mammals, some amphibians and reptiles can be closely observed. Instead of fleeing, a harmless hog-nosed snake might coil and treat us to a lively threat display followed by its death act. A tiny bright green treefrog crouched on a green leaf, relying on its cryptic coloration to escape detection, usually remains motionless while we observe it. We also enjoy hearing frogs and toads, as their breeding choruses rival the cry of the loon for enhancing a North Woods night.

gray treefrog

foxsnake

If you familiarize yourself with the snakes inhabiting the North Woods, it will cause you less anxiety when you encounter one. Instead of trying to remember general rules about distinguishing a venomous snake from a harmless one, you can just say, "It's only a foxsnake."

Amphibians and reptiles are significant strands in the North Woods food web. We obviously benefit when an army of frogs is snapping up pesky insects, or when snakes help control populations of mice and voles. In a different role, amphibians and reptiles, especially in the form of frogs, tadpoles and turtle eggs, are important food sources of many species of wildlife.

Amphibians have been recognized as being valuable indicators of environmental health. With their unshelled eggs and permeable skin, amphibians are more susceptible to pollution and other environmental deterioration than most other animals. Also, because most amphibians have life cycles that require living both in water and on land, they are vulnerable to problems with either habitat. There is a good chance that a new, unexpected environmental threat would impact amphibians first, giving us a warning signal before we are affected.

Maybe the best reason to be interested in amphibians and reptiles is that they are just plain interesting!

What Are Amphibians and Reptiles?

Amphibians and reptiles are very different groups of animals, but they also have much in common.

Amphibians and reptiles are ectothermic or cold-blooded, meaning they do not regulate body temperature internally as do the endothermic birds and mammals. Instead, amphibians and reptiles control their body temperature behaviorly by changing locations or even their postures while sunning. Reptiles may frequently move in and out of the sun to maintain an optimum body temperature. For a lizard that's been out in the sun for a while, it seems inappropriate to call it cold-blooded, so ectothermic is a better term. Amphibians spend less effort regulating body temperature, because their moist skin is better maintained in cool, moist places.

The cold climate of the North Woods forces amphibians and reptiles (except for a couple aquatic salamanders) into hibernation (sometimes called brumation for amphibians and reptiles) for roughly half the year. Various survival methods are used. Some frogs and turtles retreat to the bottom of the lake or river. Some snakes gather at hibernaculums, such as dens on southwest-facing slopes. Other snakes use anthills or crayfish burrows. Many amphibians just find shelter individually. Most species retreat below the frost level, while a few have actually adapted enough to survive freezing temperatures.

Crawling, hopping, slithering or other amphibian and reptile locomotion doesn't cover a lot of ground very fast, and the home territory of any individual is not large. Similarly, the geographic range of any species is fairly well defined and not rapidly expanded.

Most amphibians and reptiles periodically shed their outer layer of skin to accommodate growth, a process called ecdysis. Some shed the whole skin at once, while others shed it in pieces.

On the vertebrate evolutionary scale, amphibians and reptiles are above the fish and below the birds and mammals. Amphibians and reptiles have obvious external differences; amphibians have no scales or bony plates, toes are not clawed and the skin is moist or slimy. Reptiles have scales or bony plates, claws on most toes and normally dry skin.

Herpetology

The study of amphibians and reptiles is called herpetology, from the Greek word *herpeton*, which means to creep or crawl. Herpetology buffs have coined and regularly use several colloquial offshoots; herpetofauna or herps are amphibians and reptiles, herping is searching for them and herpetoculture emphasizes pets and captive breeding. Obviously it's easier to say "herps" than "amphibians and reptiles". It's certainly easier to type!

Classification of Herps

To better understand the evolutionary and current relationships of our North Woods amphibians and reptiles, it helps to know how they are classified. Every organism, living or extinct, is placed into categories based on structural similarities or differences with other organisms. This process is called taxonomy. The taxonomic system used today was devised in 1735 by the Swedish scientist, Karl von Linne', better known by his Latinized name, Carolus Linnaeus. He also began a system of binomial nomenclature, assigning a unique pair of Latin names to every species of animal and plant. The pair of Latin names, called the scientific name, identifies the species to scientists, regardless of what language they speak.

Consider the Spotted Salamander. Along with every other animal on the planet, the Spotted Salamander is in the kingdom Animalia. Animals are divided into about 35 groups called phyla. The Spotted Salamander is in the phylum Chordata, which contains all the mammals, birds, reptiles, amphibians and fish, all of which have a spinal cord. Chordata is divided into seven classes: Mammalia, Aves, Reptilia, Amphibia and three classes of fish. The class Amphibia, which includes the Spotted Salamander, is divided into orders. Salamanders are in the order Caudata, which is divided into families. The Spotted Salamander is in the family Ambystomatidae, which is the group of salamanders called mole salamanders, because they burrow and usually live underground. Families are divided into genera, with the Spotted Salamander given the genus name *Ambystoma*. Genus names are always italicized and the first letter is always capitalized. Two other North Woods salamanders are closely related and have the same genus name. Different species names, also italicized, finally distinguish them. The Spotted Salamander is *Ambystoma maculatum*, which is its scientific name.

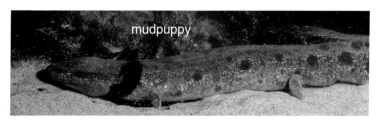

mudpuppy

Meet the Amphibians

Amphibian is a combination of two Greek words: *amphi* meaning double and *bios* meaning life. As the name states, many amphibian species lead two lives; first as an aquatic form breathing with gills, and then as a terrestrial form breathing with lungs. But there are many exceptions to this generalization.

Amphibians evolved from fish about 350 million years ago, and modern amphibians appeared about 200 million years ago. Today's amphibians

gray treefrog

either remain in water all their lives, live on land at least part of their lives, or live on land all their lives. But even the latter have not escaped the need for a moist environment.

Amphibians are characterized by their moist skin, which is susceptible to desiccation because there is no protective covering of scales, feathers or hair to help retain moisture. An amphibian's skin might not look impressive, but it's actually very specialized. The skin is permeable and absorbs water. It's a breathing organ, even though most amphibians have lungs. Amphibian skin is loaded with tiny glands, which produce substances of varying toxicity or at least give a bitter taste to a would-be predator. The skin of some amphibians displays bright warning colors to deter potential predators, while the skin of others provides camouflage. Some amphibians can change skin color to match their environment.

Two orders of amphibians inhabit the North Woods: Caudata—the salamanders, and Anura—the frogs and toads.

Amphibian Biology 101

Amphibians, as might be expected by their moist skin and jelly-like eggs, need moist conditions for breeding, usually in the form of a pond. Male amphibians have no copulatory organs, so fertilization of eggs is either indirectly internal, as in most salamanders, or external, as in frogs and toads.

Salamander Reproduction

Most North Woods salamanders emerge from hibernation with the first good rain during late March or early April. The rain, ideally an electrical storm lasting into the night, acts as a wake up call to the salamanders and synchronizes their migration to a breeding pond.

Some salamanders require fishless ponds, otherwise the adult salamanders, the eggs and the salamander larvae end up as fish food. A pond shallow enough to freeze out fish, or a vernal pond, which is a temporary spring pond formed by melting snow and spring rains, is a necessity for these salamanders. Vernal ponds usually dry by mid or late summer, which is a good reason for early breeding, to give the larvae more time to metamorphose and get out.

The indirect internal fertilization of salamander eggs is preceded by courtship, which is primarily rubbing and nudging between the male and female. The male deposits spermatophores, which are jelly-like structures capped by a packet of sperm. The female picks up spermatophores or just the sperm packet with the lips her

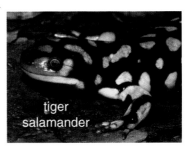

tiger salamander

cloaca, which is the chamber used for reproduction or elimination of wastes. The sperm is stored in the spermatheca, located within the female's cloaca, until she lays the eggs, which depending on the species could be a few minutes, a couple days or several months. When the eggs pass through the cloaca, they are fertilized. Salamander eggs laid in water hatch into carnivorous larvae. Salamander larvae have obvious gills, elongated bodies and have similar sized front and rear legs. A larva metamorphosing into a terrestrial adult will lose its gills and the fin from its tail. Some salamanders lay eggs on land, skipping the aquatic larvae stage.

Spotted Salamander Life Cycle

Spotted Salamanders are very early breeders, migrating during a rainy night in late March or April from their wooded upland hibernation sites. They are often a couple days behind the Blue-spotted Salamanders, which hibernate closer to the pond. Spotted Salamanders use vernal pools or other shallow, fishless waters for breeding. The males arrive first and hang out in groups called congresses. The females usually arrive a few hours later, but could be delayed for days if the rain ends quickly.

A male and female perform a dance-like courtship on the bottom of the pond, as they circle each other and nudge the base of each other's tail. Eventually the male will swim off with the female following. He then

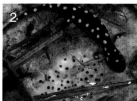

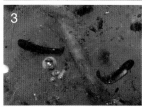

Life cycle of the Spotted Salamander.
1. Adult
2. Female with egg mass.
3. Newly-hatched larvae in "jelly."
4. Fully developed larva.
5. Newly metamorphosed salamander.

deposits a spermatophore, a jelly-like blob capped by a sperm packet, onto a leaf or twig on the pond bottom. The female moves over the sperm packet and takes it into her cloaca. Males deposit several spermatophores, and females may pick up more than one, not necessarily from the same male. She retains the sperm for a day or two. Then the sperm will fertilize the eggs as she lays them.

The female finds a stem or thin branch near the surface and lays her eggs on it. The eggs and a jelly-like substance swell to the size of a tennis ball, leaving the eggs embedded within the firm clear or milky white material. The eggs may turn green from algae in a symbiotic relationship, where the algae gets carbon dioxide from the egg and the egg gets oxygen generated by the algae. It takes the eggs about three weeks to two months to hatch, depending on water temperature. The temperature of the water also affects development of the carnivorous larvae, which need at least a couple months to develop. They usually metamorphose in late summer. A drying pond will stimulate faster development. If necessary, the larvae can overwinter in permanent bodies of water. Metamorphosis to the terrestrial form means the tail fin and gills are lost, and breathing is achieved with lungs. Newly metamorphosed salamanders stay near the pond for a while, hiding under leaves and logs. On a rainy September night they migrate to the wooded uplands. Males are mature after two or three years and females after three to five years.

Frog and Toad Reproduction

Some species of frogs breed in early spring, often using the same vernal ponds as early breeding salamanders. Other species of anurans breed later in the spring and still others breed during summer. The frogs that procrastinate until summer to breed don't need to hurry. They breed in permanent waters, and the tadpoles can overwinter before metamorphosing the next year or even two years later.

Male frogs and toads vocalize to attract a female. Each species has its own distinct call, which is made with a single vocal pouch or a pair of vocal pouches, depending on the species. Males of some species battle for territory by pushing and wrestling. A winning male becomes the resident of a prime calling site. The losers of these battles look for a different location or become satellite males. Satellite males hang around, keeping a low profile, until the resident male successfully attracts a female and moves off with her to breed. Then one of the satellite males will take his place. A satellite male might also intercept a female before she gets to the resident male. The male climbs on the female's back and clasps her behind her front legs. This embrace is called amplexus. To better maintain his grip on the female, the male has a thickened thumb during the breeding season. As she lays her eggs, he fertilizes them. Males are anxious to breed and sometimes grab another male by mistake. The grabbed male sounds a release call to point out the error. The eggs are laid in various sized clusters or strings, depending on species.

The male Spring Peeper "peeps" by inflating his single vocal pouch. He hopes to attract a mate.

The eggs hatch into tadpoles. A tadpole has a large combined head and body with a vertically flattened tail having upper and lower fins for swimming. Newly hatched tadpoles have visible gills, but these are soon covered by the opercular fold. The hidden gills still absorb oxygen as water moves through the mouth, over the gills and out the spiracle, which is a tube located on the left side of the tadpole. Tadpoles have large eyes and scraping mouth parts. They are mainly herbivorous. As tadpoles grow, the hind legs appear first, while the front legs are hidden by the opercular fold. When the front legs appear, the tadpole is close to changing to the adult form. Its tail fin disappears and the muscular portion of the tail becomes smaller. The tadpole changes from herbivore to carnivore, and it changes from breathing with gills to lungs. When this happens, the frog needs to be able to climb out of the water or it may drown. It leaves the water before the tail is completely absorbed.

The Wood Frog Life Cycle

Wood Frogs, along with spring peepers and chorus frogs, are the earliest North Woods anurans to breed. Ice may still be on the pond when warm spring rains spur the Wood Frogs to vernal pools, bogs or other small woodland wetlands.

Male Wood Frogs don't fight for territories, but they float at the surface of the water and vocalize for females. A pair of vocal pouches, one above each front leg, are rapidly inflated and deflated in a staccato, duck-like quacking call. A male seized mistakenly by another male will give out a chirp, which is the release call. A female ready to breed will allow a male to embrace her. She then swims, carrying the male on her back, to a site for laying her eggs. The male fertilizes the eggs as the female expels them where they will stick to a submerged twig or aquatic stem. The hundreds of eggs quickly absorb water and swell to a globular mass the size of a tennis ball.

Sometimes many females choose the same small area in a pond for their eggs. Possibly communal nesting offers protection from predators, because so many egg clutches in one place couldn't all be eaten before some hatch. More likely, the dark gray or black eggs warm by absorbing sunlight, and the combined effect of many clutches actually help warm the shallow pond water in that location.

The tadpoles usually hatch in two to three weeks, but the incubation time could be quicker or longer, depending on temperature. The tadpoles stay with the disintegrating egg mass for a few days before dispersing. The tadpoles have scraping mouthparts and are primarily herbivorous, eating algae and other plant matter, but they may also feed on other amphibian eggs or larvae. Many tadpoles are racing

Life cycle of the Wood Frog.
1. Vocalizing male.
2. Mating pair in amplexus.
3. Egg mass.
4. Tadpole.
5. Newly metamorphosed frog.

the season, because their pond will dry. Some years the tadpoles don't have enough time and die when the pond dries. If the pond retains water long enough, the tadpoles develop front legs in addition to the rear legs, lose their internal gills and tail fin, and the tail begins to be absorbed. The tiny frog crawls out of the water.

The new batch of Wood Frogs leaves the area around the pond and disperses into the woods. The little Wood Frogs, like the adults, are now strictly carnivorous, feeding on insects and other invertebrates. Males reach maturity in one or two years, while females require two or three years.

Meet the Reptiles

Reptiles evolved from amphibians about 335 million years ago with innovations to survive in a drier environment.

Reptiles have dry scaly skin which retains moisture and provides protection. Scales can be in various forms, from tiny granular scales to large shields. The structure of reptile scales can offer protection from predators, as in the outer covering of a turtle's shell. The color of a reptile's skin often provides camouflage. Other reptiles have warning colors. Some lizards have a brightly colored tail which acts to distract a predator. The predator grabs the tail, which promptly breaks off, and the lizard escapes.

The front foot of a reptile has five toes instead of four, and most toes have claws.

Reptiles abandoned the idea of reproducing with a gilled larval stage in a pond. Instead they have internal fertilization, which allows reptile eggs to have moisture-retaining leathery or calcareous shells. The eggs can incubate in the ground or in a moist rotting log. Some reptiles have further evolved to bear live young.

Because reptiles are ectothermic, much of their behavior involves maintaining an optimum body temperature. Turtles are especially noticeable, as they may spend hours basking in the sun. Lizards and snakes warm faster in the sun. They often move between sun and shade or warm themselves underneath a flat rock when the upper surface is too hot. Seasonal temperature changes influence when some species are nocturnal or diurnal and when they are active or dormant.

Two orders of reptiles are found in the North Woods: Testudines—the turtles, and Squamata—the lizards and snakes.

Reptile Biology 101

The reptile egg was a significant advance over jelly-like amphibian eggs, most of which require a pond. All reptiles have internal fertilization, which is a prerequisite to covering the egg with a shell. Inside the calcareous or leathery shell, a membrane called the amnion surrounds the embryo. The amnion helps retain moisture and insulate the embryo against temperature changes. Two other membranes, the chorion and allantois, contain blood vessels and are involved with oxygen transfer through the permeable shell to the developing embryo. The allantois also collects the embryo's wastes. A yolk sac supplies nutrients to the embryo.

Most reptiles are oviparous, meaning they lay eggs. All turtles are oviparous. All North Woods lizards and about half the North Woods snakes are oviparous. The other North Woods snakes bear live young. But unlike most mammals which are viviparous, the snake embryos receive no direct nourishment from the mother. Instead, each embryo has its own yolk sac. Because of this difference, live-bearing snakes are said to be ovoviviparous. When born, each juvenile snake emerges from its enclosing membrane.

Turtle Reproduction

Many North Woods turtles mate in both fall and spring. Male turtles of some aquatic species have very long front claws which are fluttered in front of the female's face and stroke the sides of her head. Courting male box turtles nip at the female's shell or feet.

A male turtle climbs the female's back and holds her shell with his claws. His longer tail twists under hers until their cloacas are in contact, and his penis can be inserted.

Turtles nest from late May into early July. Some species nest on a nearby sandbar while others travel some distance from water. The female may dig in several places before settling on the site for her eggs. In most species, the female digs a flask-shaped hole with her back feet and sometimes voids water to moisten the soil. The eggs are deposited into the nest. The female uses her back feet to cover the nest and may even crawl over it to complete the task.

Most turtle nests are dug up and destroyed by skunks, raccoons, foxes or other predators. Sometimes the predator doesn't even wait for the turtle to finish. One night I observed a Blanding's Turtle nesting and I moved on. Returning later, I found a badger, the upside-down turtle and an empty nest.

The turtles hatch in late summer. The egg is sliced open by a sharp, pointed, tooth-like structure on the turtle's snout called a caruncle. The hatchlings dig together to the surface. But the turtles of many nests overwinter there and don't emerge until spring.

Painted Turtle Life Cycle

The male Painted Turtle swims backwards in front of the female and strokes the sides of her head and neck with his long front claws. If she is receptive she strokes his front legs. The male swims around behind and then over the female and holds onto her carapace. He twists his tail under hers and they sink to the bottom of the pond. In late May or June the female crawls ashore and looks for a nesting site. She uses her back feet to dig the flask-shaped hole, often wetting the soil to soften it for digging. She lays 3 to 20, usually 7 to 9, elliptical eggs. She scrapes the excavated soil back into the nest and smooths it over. She returns to the pond. Most likely, her eggs will be devoured by a predator the first night or two. If they beat the odds, they hatch in 50 to 80 days. The sex of the hatchlings was previously determined by their incubation temperature at a certain critical time. If it was 75 to 80 degrees, all hatchlings are males. If it was 86-90 degrees, all are females. The hatchlings may stay in the nest until spring. Although subjected to freezing temperatures, the little turtles are protected by a natural antifreeze. But they may not survive extremely cold weather combined with lack of snow cover. In spring, usually after a soaking rain softens the soil, the little turtles crawl out and head for the pond. Those lucky enough to elude predators reach adult size in 4 to 6 years.

Life cycle of the Painted Turtle.
1. Female looks for egg-laying site.
2. Laying eggs in soft soil.
3. Hatching from egg.
4. Hatchling turtle.

Lizard Reproduction

Most lizards are territorial. Breeding colors and behaviors, such as head-bobbing, help establish territories and identify potential mates or intruding males. When a male finds a receptive female, he grasps her neck in his jaws and she raises her tail slightly. The male will move the base of his tail against hers. Male lizards are equipped with paired copulatory organs called hemipenes. The male inserts one hemipenis into the female during mating. Most lizards lay eggs, and some tend the eggs until they hatch.

Five-lined Skink Life Cycle

In spring, the male Five-lined Skink develops a bright red-orange coloration around his nose and mouth. He establishes and defends a territory about 30 yards in diameter. Female and juvenile skinks lack the orange-red coloration. Also, females have a bluish tail and juveniles have a bright metallic blue tail. They are allowed in the male's territory. Intruding males are driven away. The male holds the female's neck in his jaws, twists his tail under hers and inserts one hemipenis into her cloaca. The female becomes noticeably distended with eggs during early summer. She lays 5 to 18 eggs in a moist place under a log or in a burrow. She stays to tend the eggs. She basks in the sun and then warms the eggs by curling around them. By urinating in the nest, she adds humidity. She turns the eggs. If an egg spoils, she eats it. She guards the eggs from small predators. In 24 to 55 days the eggs hatch. The young, with their vivid stripes and metallic blue tails will be guarded by the mother for a day or two until they disperse.

Life cycle of the Five-lined Skink.
1. Female in burrow.
2. Eggs are guarded by the female.
3. Emerging from the egg.
4. Juvenile has a bright blue tail.

Snake Reproduction

Most snakes breed in spring or fall when they are gathered in or around their hibernaculum. The male snake can also track a female using his tongue and Jacobson's organ to sense her pheromones. Sexual recognition is by scent, since there are no obvious differences in appearance. Some male snakes engage in a form of combat, in which they wrap around each other while trying to raise above the rival and then push him down. Most male snakes will move with a jerking motion when along side a potential mate. Sometimes a rippling motion travels along his body from head to tail. Like the lizards, the male snake usually grasps the female's neck in his mouth. The snakes wrap their bodies around each other and the male uses a hemipenis for internal fertilization. Depending on species, the female lays eggs in late June or July, or bears live young in August or September. Snakes that hatch from eggs have a special egg tooth to slice open the leathery shell.

Milksnake Life Cycle

Milksnakes mate after emerging from hibernation or later in the spring. The male puts his head on top of the female and wraps his body against hers. He might hold her neck in his mouth. When their cloacas are together he inserts a hemipenis. In early July the female Milksnake lays 5 to 24 eggs in a hidden, warm, moist cavity under a rock or rotting log. The eggs stick together in a cluster, possibly as protection from being eaten by another snake. The eggs get no more protection from the female, because she abandons them. They hatch in 6 to 9 weeks. The juvenile Milksnakes are more colorful than the adults, especially when, a few days after hatching, they shed for the first time. They reach maturity in their third or fourth year.

Life cycle of the Milksnake.
1. Adult Milksnake.
2. Female with her egg cluster.
3. Juvenile cuts shell with egg tooth.
4. Hatching from the egg.

Finding and Observing

Decades ago I was looking for my first Western Foxsnake. It was mid May and I was on an abandoned railroad embankment that ran through wetlands. I heard a buzzing sound. It could have been an insect, but I looked closer. I spotted the source; a vibrating foxsnake tail. My eye moved from the tail up the body and there it was—a Western Foxsnake half coiled and basically in plain sight. Its light brown body with dark brown blotches was perfect camouflage for the heavy gravel substrate. Later that day I found another foxsnake blending into a similar background.

There are a number of lessons here. I knew what I was looking for, what it looked like and that it might buzz its tail. I knew the foxsnake's habitat and that mid May would be a good time to find one warming itself in the sun. Also, in mid May the area isn't overgrown with vegetation. After finding the second one, I was convinced that you can develop an eye for spotting the color and pattern of a species.

A cold spring pond is as unexplored as the wildest woods; get out and explore for herps.

The lesson I didn't learn then, was that once you grab the herp, you can no longer observe it in the wild. More recently, I saw a Wood Turtle walking along the sandy bottom of a shallow, clear stream. It stopped as it seemed to see me. I didn't move. The turtle scooped sand with its front feet and flipped it up onto its carapace. Then it moved closer, poked its head out of the water and looked at me. Did it feel safer—better camouflaged—with the sand on its back? I've also seen Wood Turtles on shore flip sand up on the carapace. Wood Turtles have concentric ridges on their carapace scutes. Did the ridges evolve to help hold sand grains for camouflage? More observation is needed.

The first thing to remember about finding amphibians and reptiles is to be alert for them, whether you're driving down the highway or hiking through the woods. When hiking, move slow and look close. Many herps will just freeze, relying on cryptic coloration while waiting for you to pass by. Binoculars are useful for observing and identifying turtles out on logs and to spot less obvious turtles, frogs and water snakes along the shore.

One of the best ways to find amphibians and reptiles, especially lizards and snakes, is to look under objects such as flat rocks, boards, sheets of tin and logs. Lift the object from the far side and pull it towards you, as a precaution against venomous snakes or wasps. If you lift up a flat rock that's in the sun, feel the underside. Is it slightly warm? Is it too hot for a reptile? If it's too hot, lift thicker rocks, or next time try earlier in the day.

When you lift objects, always replace them as you found them. That is home for many creatures. The rock may cover burrow entrances for invertebrates and possibly herps as well. It's inexcusable to ruin that microhabitat, which may have taken years to develop. Always be careful to avoid damage to the environment.

Search for herps at night with a good flashlight or headlamp. Some snakes and lots of amphibians will be out at night. Check around porch lights, campground lights or lit signs for opportunistic anurans devouring attracted insects.

Frogs and toads are best found at their breeding ponds. Knowing what the frog looks like and what it sounds like will make it easier to find. It helps to know how big a frog is or if it could be calling from up on a branch or from under the water. Calls can be learned from recordings listed in the back of this book.

Night is the best time to approach and observe frogs. A warm, wet night is best, because the frogs tend to come out and perch in more obvious places. The frog chorus should be enthusiastic and quick to resume if disturbed. Some frogs can be observed from the shore, but you'll see more if you enter the pond. Rubber boots help, but chest waders allow you to kneel down in one or two feet of water and be close to the frogs.

The best way to observe frogs calling is to wade into their midst, turn off your flashlight and wait for them to resume calling. When the chorus is going strong again, turn on your light and search. If you're looking for chorus frogs or Spring Peepers, don't be fooled by their decibel level. These frogs are barely over an inch long and are cryptically colored. You'll probably spot the bright vocal pouch first. Besides looking for individual vocalizing male frogs, look all around you. Females don't call. Frogs in amplexus aren't calling. Right next to you might be a species not yet breeding. A salamander or snake might be there also.

Amphibians and reptiles are amazing creatures that have been around for a very long time. I'm sure there are still many things about them we don't know. I would urge people to resist the temptation to grab, and instead, see what can be learned from observing amphibians and reptiles in the wild.

Seasonal Guide to Herps in the North Woods*

Winter: Good luck. If you can find a small place at the edge of a lake that's kept free of ice by a spring, you might find newts. You might catch a mudpuppy while ice fishing with worms.

Early April: Warm rain would spur the night migration of mole salamanders.

Mid April: Look for mole salamanders on a rainy night if they didn't run earlier. Listen especially for Wood Frogs, because their breeding season is short. Chorus frogs and Spring Peepers also start calling.

Late April: Mole salamanders may still migrate in the north. Northern Leopard Frogs join the choruses of Wood Frogs, chorus frogs and Spring Peepers. Look for basking Painted, Spotted and Blanding's Turtles. Look for gartersnakes at south-facing den sites.

Early May: Spring Peepers and Northern Leopard Frogs are still calling. Toads calling. Hatchling Painted Turtles that overwintered in the nest are on roads. Even at 55mph you can see the lumbering gait compared to a still rock. Adult turtles are basking in large numbers.

Mid May: Treefrogs are calling. Most snakes are out. Check under logs surrounding vernal ponds for salamanders.

Late May: Treefrogs calling. Four-toed Salamanders guarding eggs. Snakes migrating.

June: Treefrogs and Green Frogs calling. Turtles nesting. Look for Red-backed Salamanders foraging in the woods on wet nights. Look for mudpuppy eggs attached underneath large submerged rocks.

July: American Toad juveniles on pond shores. Red-backed Salamanders guarding eggs.

August: Look for juvenile treefrogs on tall grass or milkweeds surrounding ponds or marshes.

September: Newly metamorphosed mole salamanders migrating on rainy nights. Turtles hatching. Snakes migrating across roads.

October: Snakes at dens (hibernaculums).

*Spring may come early or late and cold spells can delay events. The order of events is a better guideline than the dates.

Photography of Herps

Photography is a great way to document some of your amphibian and reptile sightings, especially if you find a rare species or observe an interesting behavior. But more than documentation, you want quality photographs that are tack sharp, colorful and pleasing to the eye. There are many tips, techniques and equipment options that can help improve your photography of amphibians and reptiles. The first step is to understand how your camera works and how you can adjust it to produce the images you want.

Basic Photo Equipment

The Camera Body

The best camera system to use for amphibians and reptiles is a single lens reflex (SLR) camera body with interchangeable lenses. This type of cam-

The author in his night frog photography gear.

era body has a mirror inside that allows you to focus and compose your picture by looking through the lens. When the shutter release is pressed, the mirror lifts out of the way and the shutter curtain opens and closes. The time the shutter curtain is open is called the exposure time, during which light from the image hits the film or the digital sensor. A good camera body should offer you the option of switching to manual exposure, and it should have an exposure compensation dial. A good camera should allow you to use a flash with an off-camera cord.

Lenses

Lenses come in various sizes which have different uses in herp photography. A zoom lens is handy because it covers a range of lens sizes.

Wide-angle lenses such as 24mm or 28mm allow a wide view and can be used for photographing the habitat. By getting close to the herp, you can photograph it and include the habitat at the same time.

The 100mm macro lens is the most important lens for photographing herps. It focuses close, allowing you to fill the frame with such things as a baby turtle, a small frog or a turtle's face. The 100mm macro is better than a 50mm macro, because you get twice as much working distance, and the animal is less likely to bolt.

A 200mm or 300mm telephoto is great for animals that are a little farther away, such as medium to large snakes or adult turtles on land. A 400mm or 600mm lens captures images of basking turtles and other distant herps.

A 2x or 1.4x teleconverter may sometimes be useful to increase the power of your telephoto. Placed between your camera body and lens, a 2 x teleconverter effectively turns a 400mm lens into an 800mm lens. To minimize the loss of quality, only use the brand that matches your lens.

An extension tube can be a useful accessory, and because there's no glass, it's inexpensive. It attaches between your lens and camera body and allows the lens to focus closer. If you can't afford a macro lens, buy a large extension tube.

Flash

Many amphibians and reptiles are small and need to be photographed from close range. If the flash is sitting on top of the camera, it will simply miss the animal. You need on off-camera cord connecting the flash to the camera, so you can aim the flash at the subject and from the angle of your choice. Flash brackets are available which attach to the camera and hold the flash in position.

Tripod

Do you need a tripod? When using a flash, you don't need a tripod, because the flash will illuminate the object fast enough to negate any camera movement. With natural light, a general guideline says you can handhold a 100mm lens with a shutter speed of at least 1/125th of a second and a 300mm lens if your shutter speed is at least 1/300th of a second.

If you want to photograph basking turtles out your vehicle window, rest your long lens on a beanbag. Window mounts are made for this purpose, but I prefer the beanbag.

But a tripod is a vital tool for photography. Available light is frequently not sufficient for handholding a camera. Long lenses need a sturdy base but even short lenses for an animal close to you are best used with a tripod. Sometimes exposures of over a second are necessary. Having the camera on a tripod allows you to double check the exact location of your subject in the frame and gives you time to notice a distraction at the edge that you could eliminate. Using a tripod makes it easier to wait for a turtle to raise its head or a snake to flick out its tongue.

A good tripod for herps has a ball head and legs that spread wide so it can sit close to the ground. A tripod is easier to use with a quick-release system, which eliminates the annoying procedure of screwing the bolt into the camera. Basically, a quick-release plate attached to the bottom of the camera body fits into a matching clamp on the tripod. Plates are also made to fit large lenses.

Basic Photography

Exposure

Most cameras will automatically give you proper exposure for most subjects (exceptions later). Proper exposure means the photo isn't too dark and it isn't too light. Two important factors determine proper exposure, and you have to decide which is more important: aperture or shutter speed.

Aperture is the opening that allows light through the lens. The size of the aperture can be changed, and the different sizes are measured in f-stops. Basic f-stop numbers are: f/22, f/16, f/11, f/8, f/5.6, f/4 and f/2.8 (some lenses have additional or fewer numbers). The largest number indicates the smallest aperture. Because f/22 is the smallest aperture, it lets in the least amount of light which results in a long shutter speed. At the opposite end of the scale, f/2.8 is a large aperture, letting in lots of light and providing a fast shutter speed. This relationship between f/stop and shutter speed is necessary to get a properly exposed photo. The same exposure can be made from a little light for a long time, or lots of light for a short time. That's why every time you change the aperture, the shutter speed changes too. Some of the basic shutter speeds on your camera are (in seconds): 1/8, 1/16, 1/32, 1/60, 1/125, 1/250 and 1/500. If f/22 equals a shutter speed of 1/8th of a second, then opening up one stop to f/16 doubles the shutter speed to 1/16th. Opening up another stop to f/11 doubles the shutter speed again to 1/32nd. Jumping ahead, f/2.8 = 1/500th of a second. Aperture and shutter speed are inexorably linked. Every time you change from one f-stop to the next, you either double or halve the shutter speed. If you change the shutter speed, the f-stop changes in response.

Automatic exposure isn't always correct exposure. Sometimes you will have to add light or subtract light to get the correct exposure. Your camera wants to produce a medium-toned image—not too dark and not too light. Many things in nature are medium-toned or close to it, so usually the camera is automatically correct. But some animals are lighter or darker than medium-tone. If you are photographing a really dark turtle, you want your photo to show the same dark tone. If you photograph an albino herp, you don't want a photo showing a gray animal. Watch out for the background if your animal only occupies a small portion in the frame. Sand can be bright, but the camera will want it medium-toned and make your whole image too dark. Background can make a big difference when shooting with a flash. If you shoot a treefrog on a thin branch, what is the background? If it's black nothing, your treefrog will be too bright, because the camera's light meter is reading a big area.

To fix these exposure problems, your camera should have an exposure compensation dial. This is where you override your camera's auto-exposure. You might see numbers like -.5, -1, -1.5 or -2 for subtracting light, and numbers like +.5, +1, +1.5 and +2 for adding light. Other cameras compensate in 1/3rds instead. Those numbers refer to stops of light.

How much light should you add or subtract? If you have a digital camera, just shoot, look at your image, adjust and shoot again. If you're shooting film, aim at a medium-tone subject in the same light and see what the exposure would be. Then aim at your subject and notice the difference. That will tell you how much to compensate. If you want to be sure, then bracket the exposure by shooting a half stop over and a half stop under your best guess.

Sharpness and Depth of Field

Using flash will freeze movement and produce sharp photos.

With natural light, shutter speed obviously affects the sharpness of photos, because at slow shutter speeds, movement of camera or subject will create a blur.

Proper focus is necessary to get sharp photos. Focus on the eye of the animal. If the eye isn't sharp, the photo is no good. Don't use autofocus for amphibians and reptiles. Autofocus doesn't know an eye from a tail, and when you photograph turtles out on a log, you want the turtles to be sharp, not the ripples in the water.

Sharpness includes the depth of field in a photo. Depth of field refers to how much of your photo appears in sharp focus and how much is blurred. It's the zone of sharpness front to back in the image. When you photograph an amphibian or reptile, you want the whole animal sharp, not just the eye and part of its body. Remember those f-stop numbers? Guess what? They determine depth of field. The widest depth of field is obtained by using the smallest aperture, which was f/22. Unfortunately, that aperture gives the slowest shutter speed. You'll be constantly dealing with the trade-off of shutter speed versus depth of field. Frequently you'll be forced to use a tripod or flash to avoid blur produced by narrow depth of field or movement.

Composition

Composition is the arrangement of the subject and other elements within your photo to create a more interesting or pleasing appearance. There are some general rules of composition to consider when taking a photograph. The first decision is whether a vertical or horizontal format would work best. An amphibian or reptile just sitting there usually works best as a horizontal. But when a snake or turtles raises it head up, or a treefrog is vertical on a branch, a vertical picture might work better.

The rule of thirds is frequently used to compose an image. Divide the picture into thirds with tic-tac-toe lines. Where the lines intersect is often the best location to place your subject or the animal's eye. A subject positioned dead center is often boring. If you photograph a horizontal log with a bunch of turtles on it, place it on the lower thirds line rather than across the center.

When you photograph an animal, there should be more room in front of the animal than behind it. Give the critter room to jump or crawl, rather than placing it like it's already leaving.

Be aware of lines within the photo. Lines should lead your eye into the picture, not out of it. Diagonal lines are more dynamic than horizontal or vertical lines.

Use elements in the photo to frame your subject.

Simplify! Get rid of unnecessary clutter. Avoid distracting bright hotspots in the background.

Natural Light

Photographers usually avoid the harsh light of the midday sun, but the best time to photograph an amphibian or reptile is whenever you find one. Many reptiles bask in bright sun. If possible the warm sunlight of early morning or late afternoon is much better. On a sunny blue sky day, beware of photographing in the shade because of the blue tint.

Overcast or cloudy bright days are great for photographing herps.

Night Photography

Most of my night photography is amphibians, either in a pond or in wet woods. Most photography is at close range, so the flash should be off the hot shoe, attached with a cord. I don't like using a flash bracket, because I'll want to change the flash angle quickly.

I use the bright adjustable beam of a three cell Maglite to search for amphibians. When not needed, it drops into an accessory belt holder or into the leg pocket of cargo pants. A headlamp is useful but it gets in the way of the camera. When actually photographing, I use a Rayovac Workhorse to illuminate the amphibian. It's small, using two AA batteries and its flattened shape allows it to be rubber banded to the top of my flash. Now the camera is in one hand, while the flash and flashlight, both aimed at the amphibian, are in the other.

For the pond, chest waders are far superior to any boots. Your back will prove that the first time you try to photograph a frog in a foot of water, while trying to keep your boots from flooding. A photo vest or some kind of pouch is needed to hold the bulky flash/flashlight combo while searching for frogs. I think dark or camouflage colored clothing is less disturbing to frogs. A hat with a strap will stay on your head and ward off mosquitoes.

Amphibian & Reptile Photo Tips

My favorite way to photograph herps is in the wild, natural and untouched, exactly as I find them. The next best thing is to photograph the amphibian or reptile on location even though the rock or log no longer covers it. Sometimes an animal in tall grass or bushes has to be placed in the open or a snake is encouraged to coil to better fit in the frame.

Before grabbing any amphibian or reptile, make sure it's legal. All herps are protected in some parks and refuges, and some species are protected everywhere. Never grab an amphibian with insect repellent on your hands, due to its porous skin and sensitivity to chemicals.

Try to have your camera ready. You may have only moments before a discovered critter zips into the bush. When you find a subject, get a couple record shots. Gradually move in and improve your photos. When you think you're close enough, look to improve the photo. Is there an ugly brown leaf partially in the way? Maybe you can use a stick to move it without scaring the animal. Maybe a different angle would be better.

If you want photos of amphibians and reptiles in the wild, don't go with a bunch of overzealous herpers. They tend to race ahead and grab everything. It's difficult trying to get a quality photo, while listening to the excitement of the next discovery up the trail.

Salamanders are often hidden under logs and some of them will sit still for a picture after the log is turned. If a salamander constantly crawls, give it a little piece of bark to hide under and wait a couple minutes for it to settle down. Then pull the bark away and shoot. A salamander can be placed in a suitable spot a few times but don't persist. Be sure to replace both log and salamander.

Frogs at the edge of a pond can often be approached close for photos. Keep low and move slow. Elbows braced on the ground provide good camera support.

Basking turtles are often too wary to stalk. One option is drifting toward them in a boat or canoe. You'll probably have to try several, before one stays. Another option is to approach from shore and let them drop into the water. Then hide in a portable blind, like the kind that just drapes over you. Try not to feel stupid when the turtles poke their heads up and stare at you. After a few minutes some should emerge onto the log. They know you're there but since you're out of sight, they must feel safe. I was waiting for turtles once, when some that I hadn't seen returned to sunning about five feet away. Of course they were too close to photograph with the telephoto lens I was using.

Lizards are best photographed on a chilly morning, before they come out and warm up. When found underneath a flat rock or other shelter, there is a good chance a cold lizard will stay a few moments.

Snakes can be easy or impossible. If a snake coils defensively, you should be able to get a lot of good shots. When a snake persists in crawling, give it something to hide under, like a snake bag, shirt or hat. Let it relax while you pre-focus. Then pull the object off and shoot. If a snake is in thick vegetation where you can't get a photo, you can try gently moving it into the open, but be careful where you put it. Don't put a snake on a picturesque rock and expect it to stay there, if the rock has been baking in the sun. A herp will overheat and die if you keep putting it on hot surface. The health of an amphibian or reptile is always more important than a photo. Your health is important too. Don't take chances with venomous snakes! If you're photographing a rattlesnake, remember there could be another nearby. Also, have someone watching for you, because it's easy to misjudge distance while looking through a lens.

Catching and Studying

Amphibians and reptiles are studied by herpetologists who want to learn more about them and their role in the environment. One species in a designated area may be studied over time to estimate how many are there and if the population is increasing or declining. Sometimes a specific area is studied to learn what species are found there, and then which places are most important to protect. Disappearing and deformed frogs have been the focus of many studies that are still ongoing.

This Blanding's Turtle is numbered for a Minnesota tracking study.

Frog and toad population surveys are done three times a year during designated periods to include the breeding season of all anurans. The surveyor travels the same route and stops at the same breeding ponds. The species heard calling are recorded, along with an estimate of calling intensity and temperature data. Over the years, population trends can be demonstrated.

Most amphibians and reptiles have to be captured for study. A team of people may simply search an area and grab every amphibian and reptile they can find. Nets are used to capture aquatic herps, while snake hooks and snake bags are the most common terrestrial tools. In preparation for a survey, boards may be laid out at intervals in likely places. Weeks later they are checked for whatever herps might be underneath. Drift

Dan Nedrelo sets a turtle trap for a Wisconsin Departments of Natural Resources study.

fences are often used in surveys. These can be made from various materials, including rolls of thin aluminum, hardware cloth, chicken wire and the black plastic used to prevent erosion around construction sites. The drift fence is stretched out to block the path an amphibian or reptile is likely to travel while migrating or searching for a nesting site. Sometimes funnel traps are placed along the fence, or pit traps are dug at each end. The pit trap may be a jar or can with the top at ground level. A board can be placed over it, so a lizard dashing under the board will fall into the container.

Large hoop nets are used with bait to capture turtles. The nets are partly above water so the turtles can breathe.

Snakes may be caught in funnel traps or captured by hand, especially around den sites. Depending on the study, captured herps are usually marked in some way so they can be identified if recaptured later. The usual method for marking turtles is to file notches in the marginal scutes. One method of marking snakes is to insert a tiny passive implant transponder tag (PIT tag) underneath the skin. When the snake is recaptured, it can be identified with a device that scans and reads the tag through the skin. Sometimes an animal is equipped with a transmitter so it can be relocated by radio-telemetry.

Top: A Massasauga is implanted with a tiny transponder. Bottom: The same snake can be identified with the use of a scanner when recaptured.

Studying amphibians and reptiles doesn't have to be an official project. Anyone can gather data. It starts with a notebook. Whenever you find an amphibian or reptile, record the species or subspecies, sex (if known), approximate age, date, location, time of day, weather conditions and other information, such as AOR (alive on road), DOR (dead on road), basking on rock, under a log, etc. I started keeping records on herps when I was in eighth grade and I refer to some of that data nearly every year.

Conservation

Amphibians and reptiles are under siege. Most species are diminishing in numbers due to a multitude of reasons, especially environmental degradation, and, unless I'm overlooking something, all are ultimately the fault of man.

All too often, reptiles are deliberately killed. Of course snakes are killed by people who are ignorant, afraid and/or just plain ruthless. But even turtles are killed. There are actually people who deliberately drive over turtles or shoot them for target practice.

Female Snapping Turtles are especially vulnerable when searching for nesting sites.

Some people remove reptiles from the wild. A North Woods tourist finds a Wood Turtle or a Spotted Turtle, both of which are protected, and takes it home for a pet. A few reptile enthusiasts, who know better, might take one as well. These individual losses to the population add up. It takes years to replace an adult turtle, and the mortality of eggs and young is very high. But far worse is the problem with poachers taking them for the pet trade. Wood Turtles have been especially hard hit as poachers take every one they can find, literally decimating the population along some stretches of river. Wood Turtle population surveys, carried on for years where the turtles were plentiful, have been terminated because one year the turtles are missing. A few poachers have been busted for selling the turtles in other states. Box turtle populations have also been hurt.

Disappearing habitat is a serious problem for amphibians and reptiles. Development is constantly destroying habitat. Displaced animals can't simply move somewhere else, because somewhere else is usually already occupied. A habitat is limited in how many of any species can live there. That limit is called the carrying capacity. The limiting factor may be food, shelter or something else, but when the carrying capacity is reached, there is no room for more.

Wetlands are often destroyed by development. The doomed resident amphibians and reptiles don't care that five miles down the road a big hole is being dug and filled with water as a mitigation site. Vernal ponds often get filled because they are dry part of the year, but that is why some amphibians breed there. The addition of fish to a small pond is also destructive, because they devour the salamander larvae and tadpoles.

Poorly placed roads, such as through wetlands or between forest and pond, can result in high mortality of herps during migrations.

Clear-cuts doom salamanders. Even selective cutting makes the forest drier and less hospitable for amphibians.

More sinister assaults on amphibians and reptiles involve the widespread deterioration of the environment by polluting chemicals. Amphibians are especially vulnerable because their skin and unshelled eggs are exposed to water, soil and sun. Studies have shown that increased ultraviolet-B radiation, due to the thinning ozone layer, can kill amphibian eggs.

Wetlands continue to be filled, dooming the reptiles and amphibians that need them.

Frogs received a lot of publicity when large numbers were found deformed in 1995. Frogs have been found with extra legs, misplaced legs, missing legs, missing eyes and even more grotesque deformities. Some deformities are caused when the larva of a parasitic flatworm forms a cyst in the developing leg of a tadpole. But many scientists believe other factors cause deformities, as well.

Frog populations have declined or disappeared in some places. If a cause, such as disease, fungus or parasite is suspected, the real culprit may be much more complex. The frog's immune system may have been weakened first by a chemical pollutant, making the frog more susceptible.

Acid rain, PCBs, mercury, pesticides and herbicides are all threats to amphibians. Pesticides and herbicides can contaminate breeding ponds, either from drifting spray or from rainwater runoff.

Studies by Hayes showed that a widely used herbicide caused sexual abnormalities which

Green Herons are a natural hazard in the wild.

feminized male Northern Leopard Frogs. When tadpoles developed in water containing atrazine at 0.1 parts per billion (the EPA's limit for drinking water is 30 times higher!) the resulting hermaphroditic frogs had both ovaries and testes, or they had egg cells inside the testes.

Further studies by Hayes have found that combinations of commonly used pesticides, herbicides and fungicides have more severe effects than would result from the same concentration of only one.

A study by Relyea found that a commonly used herbicide, Roundup, used at the recommended amount, killed frogs and toads on land and tadpoles in the water. On land, 79% of the frogs and toads died within one day. In the water, 98% of the tadpoles died. The anurans used in the study were the American Toad, Gray Treefrog and Northern Leopard Frog.

Many of our amphibian and reptile populations are declining. Federal regulations protecting wetlands have been weakened and are still under attack. Quality habitats have been drained, filled, polluted or otherwise destroyed. A lot of people don't like politics, but politics will decide what North Woods habitats and species will still be around years from now. Anyone who cares about amphibians, reptiles and other North Woods wildlife needs to start paying attention. Some politicians care about environmental protections.

Amphibian deformities may be the result of agricultural runoff or some other environmental contaminant.

Others would sell off parks and forests to balance the budget, or drive over a vernal pond in August to show it's not much of a wetland. Know who is who. Don't listen to them; check their environmental voting records. Support organizations that protect habitat. Future generations might want to hear frogs in a pond or watch turtles on a log. What a shame if those pleasures are forever lost.

How to use this Field Guide

Amphibians and Reptiles of the North Woods is designed to make field identification easier for you, the reader. Through the use of color photos, arrows pointing to field marks, maps, phenograms and habitats, we have made a handy, compact and easy to use guide. Also, by limiting the amphibians and reptiles to those found in one geographic area, we have eliminated the need to wade through several hundred species, many of which would never be found here. Included is every regularly occurring herp in the North Woods of the Western Great Lakes.

Amphibian & Reptile Names

Like other organisms, herps are given both common and scientific names. The common names are the English names most amateur naturalists use, while the scientific or Latin names tend to be the spoken word of herpetologists. We capitalize species names but use lower case for groups (e.g. Common Gartersnakes are actually a type of gartersnake). If there is a distinct subspecies in our area, we list it. For example, there are two subspecies of Painted Turtle in the North Woods (Western Painted Turtle and Midland Painted Turtle) and we cover them both.

Taxonomy is a fluid science; names are always in a state of flux. We've decided to use the list recognized by several professional organizations. Go to *www.herplit.com/SSAR/circulars/HC29/Crother.html* and click on "PDF of Book" or Google "herplit list north america."

Photos

Nearly all photos are by the author. Many were taken in the wild but if the subjects were temporarily captive animals, Allen was careful to keep them in their natural habitat. We've attempted to show as many behaviors and stages of the species life cycle as we could. The symbol used for males is ♂ and the female symbol is ♀.

Fieldmark Arrows

Arrows point to diagnostic features in the photos that are referenced in the description text and marked with an arrow symbol (↑). These are characteristics that you should look for while in the field.

Phenograms

What is a phenogram? All amphibians and reptiles live out their lives according to seasonal timing that is characteristic for that species. Our phenogram highlights in red the time when that species is active and not hibernating. Some species, such as the Mudpuppy, are active all year. Of course, weather and latitude will cause some variation in dates.

Habitat

Preferred habitat is found beneath the phenogram. Remember, this is where courtship, mating and egg laying takes place, and the larva develops and emerges. Your best bet to find the species will probably be near such habitat—but not exclusively.

Nature Notes

Nature Notes are fascinating bits of natural history that bring one a more complete understanding of that species. Unique defense behavior, hunting techniques and diet preferences are just some of the topics touched on.

Range Map

A map of the North Woods shows the range of that species in green. This is the range as we know it from current population data but some amphibian and reptile populations are poorly understood or changing.

☐ **Species Range**

Species Text

Description covers the best distinguishing field characteristics. If males and females are different (sexual dimorphism) then these differences are described. Measurements given are the average body length in inches. For skinks, the measurement is snout-to-vent length because the tail can break off. Salamander measurements, though, are snout to end of tail. Turtle measurements are the straight-line carapace length.

If there are unique aspects to a species range that cannot be seen by the map, we list them under **Range Notes**.

Courtship, Mating & Eggs covers exactly that—except for species that bear live young (several species of snakes). Reptiles and amphibians have unique courtship rituals that are discussed here. Salamanders and frogs progress through several distinct life stages and these are covered as well.

Diet is only covered for snakes and turtles, who can have very specific prey preferences.

Glossary

Check out the glossary for easy-to-understand meanings of some tricky terms.

North Woods Herp Checklist

In Appendix A, you will find a checklist of all 46 species found in the North Woods of Minnesota, Wisconsin, Michigan and northwest Ontario. Check off the ones you see in your travels afield.

Titles of Interest

This list of recommended reading and resources includes our favorite titles for delving deeper into the fascinating world of herps. Also listed are books on close-up nature photography. **Additional References** lists other pertinent research papers and articles. You may also want to pick up a CD of frog and toad calls to better equip yourself for field identification. Several sources are listed here.

Enjoy *Amphibians and Reptiles of the North Woods*. Take it with on hikes. Stuff it in your canoe pack. Use it. But most importantly, have fun getting to know our fascinating northern herps.

Order Caudata – Salamanders

Salamanders are amphibians that have tails as adults. They have elongated bodies and most have four legs of relatively equal size. There is no tympanum. Salamanders breathe with one or more of the following organs: gills, lungs or skin. The approximately 410 species known throughout the world are grouped into ten families. In the North Woods, we have only seven species, but they represent the diversity of four families.

Family Proteidae – Mudpuppies and Waterdogs

This family has only six species worldwide. All are neotenic, keeping their gills and remaining totally aquatic through adulthood. We have a single North Woods species: Mudpuppy.

Family Salamandridae – Newts

About 55 species of newts occur worldwide. Newts are not slimy; they have drier, rougher skin than other salamanders. They are primarily aquatic with tail fins but the adults don't have gills. One species lives in our area: Eastern Newt.

Family Ambystomatidae – Mole Salamanders

There are at least 30 species of mole salamanders, which are found only in North America. These are stout medium-sized salamanders that spend most of there lives underground or at least underneath logs or other shelter. Adults have four toes on each front foot and five on each rear foot. Mole salamanders have distinct vertical creases on their sides called costal grooves that can be useful in identification. Three species are found in the North Woods: Blue-spotted Salamander, Spotted Salamander and Tiger Salamander.

Family Plethodontidae – Lungless Salamanders

This is a large family with about 266 species worldwide. These salamanders actually are lungless, breathing only through their skin and the lining of the mouth. Dependent on breathing through the skin, they are necessarily small. Members of the Plethodontidae have a unique feature called a nasolabial groove. This tiny groove runs from the nostril to the mouth and is believed to enhance the sense of smell. In some species the groove ends in a tiny projection called a cirrus that extends just below the mouth line. Cirri are sometimes more prominent in males. Two species of lungless salamanders are found in the North Woods: Four-toed Salamander and Eastern Red-backed Salamander.

Salamander Larvae Comparison

Mudpuppy

Yellowish dorsolateral stripes. Four toes on hind foot. Dorsal fin is only on the tail.

Central Newt

Two rows of dorsal light spots and a dark stripe through the eye. Five toes on hind foot. Dorsal fin nearly to head. No costal grooves.

Blue-spotted Salamander

Dark blotches on back with mottling on tail fin, irregular light lateral stripe. Toes rounded with five on hind foot. Dorsal fin nearly to head.

Spotted Salamander

No blotches on tail fin. Toes rounded with five on hind foot. Dorsal fin nearly to head.

Tiger Salamander

Dark spots on back and possible light stripe. Toes flat and pointed with five on hind foot. Dorsal fin nearly to head. Large size; up to five inches.

Four-toed Salamander

Usually has a dark bar behind the eye. Four toes on hind foot. Dorsal fin nearly to head.

Mudpuppy *Necturus maculosus*

| APRIL | MAY | JUNE | JULY | AUG | SEPT | OCT |

Rivers and large lakes. Surprisingly in both turbid slow rivers with mud bottom or in clear, fast-moving, gravel-bottomed rivers.

Meet the Mudpuppy

Nature Notes:

Mudpuppies can swim with an undulating tail motion and legs held at their sides, but usually just walk on the bottom.

Lungs are used mostly for depth regulation instead of breathing.

Mudpuppies forage mostly at night, especially in clear water. During the day they hide under rocks or logs to avoid predation.

Description: Length is 13 to 16 inches long.

The Mudpuppy is a large salamander with a vertically flattened paddle-like tail. The skin, which is exceedingly slippery and slimy, varies from brown to gray to nearly black with darker spots or blotches. They have gills, small lidless eyes and four toes on each foot.

The gills vary in appearance. Mudpuppies that live in slow moving, stagnant or warm water with less oxygen have large, red, bushy gills, while those that live in cool, fast flowing streams with plenty of oxygen have compact, darker gills.

Mudpuppies are neotenic, meaning mature adults are totally aquatic because they retain their larval characteristics, including gills.

Courtship, Mating & Eggs: Reproduction is similar to most salamanders with courtship

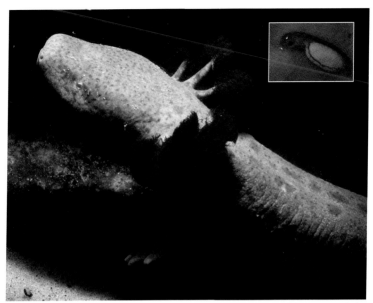

Bushy red gills are an adaptation for water low in oxygen. The gills provide much needed surface area for oxygen absorption. Insert: This is a rare photo of a Mudpuppy embryo.

followed by deposition of spermatophores which are taken into the female's cloaca. Active year-round; breed in fall and early winter. The female lays eggs in late spring or early summer. She hollows out a silt-free nesting area underneath a large flat rock or log. She attaches 18 to 190 eggs, singly, so they hang from the underside of the rock or log; she then guards them for about two months until they hatch. The Mudpuppy larval stage lasts 4 to 6 years before reaching maturity.

Nature Notes:

The Mudpuppy is the only known host for larvae of the Salamander Mussel (*Simpsonaias ambigua*). The tiny larvae clamp onto the mudpuppy's gills, form cysts, and develop there for 8 to 12 weeks. Then the cysts break, releasing the tiny mussels. All other known hosts of mussels are fish.

Note the Mudpuppy's paddle-like tail.

larval stage

The larva has yellowish back stripes, four hind toes and the dorsal fin is only on the tail.

Central Newt *Notophthalmus viridescens louisianensis*

newt stage

APRIL	MAY	JUNE	JULY	AUG	SEPT	OCT

Small ponds, shallow lakes, river backwaters and clear streams with much aquatic vegetation. Efts in woods near breeding pond.

Meet the Eastern Newt

Nature Notes:

Central Newts are day-active and forage on various invertebrates plus the eggs and larvae of other amphibians.

During winter they remain in deeper waters or water kept open by springs, but newts in shallow water bail out and hibernate on land.

Description: Length is 2½ to 4 inches.

The Central Newt is a subspecies of the Eastern Newt. It is a two-tone salamander with olive-green on the top half , yellow below and speckled all over with black. The skin is dryer than other salamanders and is not slimy. In its normal aquatic adult form, it has a tail fin but no gills. Adult males, during the breeding season, have an enlarged tail fin that extends from the tail over much of the back. The Central Newt has sharply contrasting dorsal and ventral colors and usually no red spots. Adult newts forced into a terrestrial existence by environmental conditions lose the tail fin and the skin turns darker and rough. The eft, an intermittent land stage between larva and adult, is reddish brown with rough skin.

Range Notes: In Minnesota and Wisconsin its distribution is spotty and the eft stage is rare.

eft stage

The eft is the terrestrial stage of the newt. They are most active during wet weather.

Courtship, Mating & Eggs: Active year-round. Courtship is in late fall and winter. The male will grasp the female and wave his tail, fanning his scent towards her. Then he walks in front of her and deposits a spermatophore, which she picks up and stores in her cloaca. In April, the eggs are fertilized as the female lays them. She spends several days attaching 12 to 140 eggs, usually singly, on submerged plant stems. Varying with water temperature, the eggs hatch in about a month. By the end of summer the larvae are ready to change. Some metamorphose into the terrestrial eft stage, while others, especially in Minnesota and Wisconsin, metamorphose directly into adults.

Nature Notes:

Efts are most likely found during a rain as they walk over leaf litter on the forest floor.

larval stage

The larva has two rows of dorsal light spots and a dark stripe through the eye. Five hind toes. Dorsal fin nearly to head.

Red-spotted Newt *Notophthalmus viridescens viridescens*

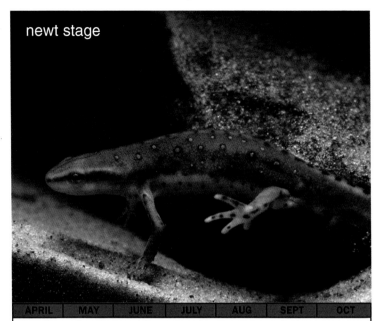

newt stage

| APRIL | MAY | JUNE | JULY | AUG | SEPT | OCT |

Small ponds, shallow lakes, river backwaters and clear streams with much aquatic vegetation. Efts in woods near breeding pond.

Meet the Red-spotted Newt

Nature Notes:

Red-spotted Newts are day-active and forage on various invertebrates plus the eggs and larvae of other amphibians.

During winter they remain in deeper waters or water kept open by springs, but newts in shallow water bail out and hibernate on land.

Description: Length is 2½ to 4 inches.

The Red-spotted Newt is a subspecies of the Eastern Newt. It has bright red spots, usually bordered by black and sometimes in two rows on the back. The skin is dryer than other salamanders and is not slimy. In its normal aquatic adult form, it has a tail fin but no gills. Adult males, during the breeding season, have an enlarged tail fin that extends from the tail over much of the back. Adult newts forced into a terrestrial existence by environmental conditions lose the tail fin and the skin turns darker and rough. The eft, an intermittent land stage between larva and adult, also has red spots and is sometimes bright orange-red.

Range Notes: In our area, only found in southeast Michigan and in Canada on the north and east sides of Lake Superior.

eft stage

The Red-spotted Newt's eft stage is sometimes bright orange. It is a subspecies of the Eastern Newt found north of Lake Superior in Ontario.

Courtship, Mating & Eggs: Active year-round. Courtship is in late fall and winter. The male will grasp the female and wave his tail, fanning his scent towards her. Then he walks in front of her and deposits a spermatophore, which she picks up and stores in her cloaca. In April, the eggs are fertilized as the female lays them. She spends several days attaching 12 to 140 eggs, usually singly, on submerged plant stems. Varying with water temperature, the eggs hatch in about a month. By the end of summer the larvae are ready to change. Some metamorphose into the terrestrial eft stage, while others, especially in Minnesota and Wisconsin, metamorphose directly into adults.

Nature Notes:

Because of its terrestrial habitat, the eft needs more protection and has more poison glands concentrated on its back than the aquatic adult.

Note the red to orange spots that give this attractive amphibian its name.

Blue-spotted Salamander *Ambystoma laterale*

APRIL	MAY	JUNE	JULY	AUG	SEPT	OCT

Forested areas that have vernal pools for breeding. Tolerant of dry woods and disturbed areas. Even under logs in summer.

Nature Notes:

The Blue-spotted Salamander can exude a white sticky substance from the skin, especially on the base of the tail, to discourage predators.

The salamander raises and waves its tail, perhaps as a warning.

Meet the Blue-spotted Salamander

Description: Length is 4 to 5½ inches.

The Blue-spotted Salamander is dark gray to nearly black with numerous small blue spots or flecks. Newly metamorphosed salamanders have yellow specks instead of blue.

Courtship, Mating & Eggs: Blue-spotted Salamanders are thought to hibernate around the edge of the breeding pond, because in early spring they often precede the Spotted Salamanders by a couple days. During courtship, the male clasps the female behind her front legs for a time before moving in front of her and depositing one to three spermatophores. She picks up the sperm packet and stores it in her cloaca for a couple days. She lays 1 to 35 eggs, attaching them singly or in small clusters to submerged twigs and

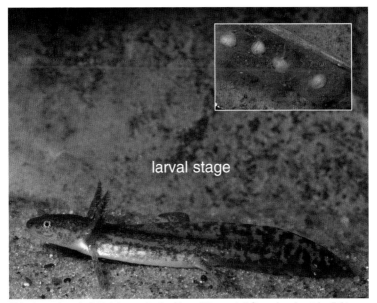

Older larva show dark blotches on back with mottling on tail fin and an irregular light stripe down each side. Toes are rounded with five on hind foot. Dorsal fin nearly to head. Inset: Blue-spotted Salamander eggs attached to a submerged twig.

leaves. The larvae hatch out in 3 to 5 weeks and metamorphose in August.

Nature Notes:

Blue-spotted Salamanders are more likely to be found under logs during summer than other mole salamanders, most of which have retreated underground.

Developing embryo inside egg.

The amount of blue spotting varies with individuals.

Spotted Salamander *Ambystoma maculatum*

| APRIL | MAY | JUNE | JULY | AUG | SEPT | OCT |

Closed-canopy deciduous or mixed forests. Vernal pools in spring are vital for reproduction.

Nature Notes:

Spotted Salamanders are rarely seen except during breeding and migration times. They spend most of the time burrowed under ground, where they keep cool, moist and well fed on worms and other invertebrates.

Must have closed-canopy forests to retain needed moisture on forest floor.

Meet the Spotted Salamander

Description: Length is 5 to 7 inches.

The Spotted Salamander is dark gray to nearly black with yellow spots loosely arranged in two rows. Some individuals have only a few spots or none at all. Often there is an orange spot behind each eye. Newly metamorphosed Spotted Salamanders are brown with tiny gold or yellow flecks.

Range Notes: Not known in Minnesota until 2001 when its egg masses were located in Pine County in the Nemadji State Forest.

Courtship, Mating & Eggs: In late March or early April, rain triggers the migration of Spotted Salamanders to their breeding ponds. Males arrive a day or two before females. Courtship precedes the deposition of spermatophores, which the female retrieves and stores in her cloaca. A day or two later she lays

The larva has no blotches on the tail fin. Toes are rounded with five on hind foot. The dorsal fin goes nearly to the head. Inset: A newly metamorphosed salamander leaves the water.

her 50 to over 250 eggs in one or more masses attached to submerged sticks or stems. After some swelling with water, the result is a tennis ball sized mass of firm clear or cloudy substance with eggs embedded inside. It holds its shape if removed from water. It takes the eggs 20 to 60 days to hatch, depending on water temperature. The larvae take at least two months to develop, with the option of overwintering if the pond doesn't dry.

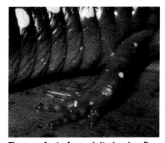

The rear foot of an adult showing five toes.

A female with her eggs.

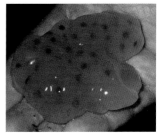

The Spotted's firm egg mass.

Tiger Salamander *Ambystoma tigrinum*

| APRIL | MAY | JUNE | JULY | AUG | SEPT | OCT |

Woods, open areas and even suburbs. Breeding areas include forest ponds, farm ponds, gravel pits and fish-rearing ponds.

Nature Notes:

There are a few populations of Tiger Salamanders in the North Woods region that are neotenic. These salamanders reach sexual maturity without metamorphosing into the adult form. They retain their gills and tail fins and remain aquatic.

Meet the Tiger Salamander

Description: Length is 7 to 8 inches. The Tiger Salamander is the largest terrestrial salamander in the North. A Minnesota specimen holds the record of 13¼ inches.

It is dark gray or black with highly variable and random yellow blotches that extend to the belly. The lower lip and throat are yellow.

Courtship, Mating & Eggs: Migrate to breeding ponds in early spring, with males arriving two or three days before the females. Courtship involves a male nudging at a female, followed by his deposition of a spermatophore and the females taking it into her cloaca. After about a day the female will lay her fertilized eggs in clusters attached to twigs, leaves or other debris near the bottom of the pond. They don't have the same firmness as those of Spotted Salamanders and fall apart when lift-

larval stage

The larva has dark spots on the back and sometimes a light stripe. Toes are flat and pointed with five on hind foot. The dorsal fin goes nearly to the head. And they are large; often reaching five inches. Inset: The same larva at a younger age.

ed. Eggs hatch in two to four weeks. In a permanent pond, the larvae can overwinter. In a drying pond, the density of salamander larvae can greatly increase. Larvae respond by speeding up their rate of development. Some larvae become cannibals. They were already carnivores, but now they develop longer heads, bigger mouths, longer teeth and proceed to devour their siblings.

Nature Notes:

Since they live underground and migrate on rainy nights, they often escape notice until they fall into someone's window well or swimming pool.

The shed skin of a molting Tiger Salamander.

Young Tiger Salamanders have fewer spots. This one is eating a worm.

Four-toed Salamander *Hemidactylium scutatum*

| APRIL | MAY | JUNE | JULY | AUG | SEPT | OCT |

Forests with wet depressions and sphagnum moss. Spring-fed swamps, spring-fed bogs and spring-fed creeks.

Nature Notes:

The Four-toed Salamander can break off its tail as a defense. The wiggling tail may distract a predator long enough for the salamander to escape. A new tail is regenerated.

Meet the Four-toed Salamander

Description: Length is 2 to 3½ inches.

The Four-toed Salamander is named for having four toes on each hind foot (most salamanders have five). This salamander has a reddish-brown back, often spotted with black. Its gray or brown sides are speckled. The base of the tail is constricted and the belly is white with black dots (see inset photo). Juveniles have darker bellies with blue dots. Newly metamorphosed Four-toed Salamanders have a short dark stripe behind each eye.

Range Notes: This species was first discovered in Minnesota in 1994, when found in Itasca County. In 1999, more were found in Aitkin, Carlton, Mille Lacs and Pine Counties. St. Louis County has since been added to the list. These discoveries were made by Carol Hall and her Minnesota County Biological Survey teams.

The larva usually has a dark bar behind the eye. Four toes on hind foot. The dorsal fin goes nearly to the head. Inset left: Eggs are laid in sphagnum moss that overhangs the water (inset right) or mounds at the base of willows and alder.

Courtship, Mating & Eggs: Courtship takes place during fall or spring. The male rubs his nose and chin against the female's snout. The female straddles the male's tail and nudges the base of his tail. The male deposits a spermatophore, which is picked up and stored in the female's cloaca. During spring, the female migrates to a site for her eggs. The ideal situation has sphagnum moss overhanging shallow, spring-fed waters. If not actually overhanging the water, there must be ground vegetation or a rotted log next to the water. The female, in a small hollow, turns upside down and lays a cluster of 15 to 64 eggs. The eggs stick to each other and to the ceiling of the hollow. The female guards them for 38 to 60 days until the eggs hatch. The hatchling larvae drop into the water or wriggle until gravity helps them get there. They need three to eight weeks to transform into the terrestrial form.

Nature Notes:

Very secretive and difficult to find. Their habitat requirements severely limit where they can survive, and even in optimum habitats they are never plentiful.

Sphagnum moss is an essential habitat requirement.

Eastern Red-backed Salamander *Plethodon cinereus*

APRIL	MAY	JUNE	JULY	AUG	SEPT	OCT

Forests with closed canopy and leaf litter, rotting logs or moss. Terrestrial; Does not need standing water for breeding.

Nature Notes:

Red-backed Salamanders are territorial. Both male and female will defend their territory, probably as a defense of their food source.

The salamander raises its body off the ground to threaten an intruder. The threat is increased when it raises its tail also. If necessary, it bites at the intruding Red-backed's nasolabial groove or tail to drive it away.

Meet the Eastern Red-backed Salamander

Description: Length is 2½ to 4 inches.

The Eastern Red-backed Salamander is small and has small legs with five toes on each hind foot. Most the North Woods specimens are the "redback" color phase, with a brick red color straight down the back and onto the tail. The sides and belly are gray with light and dark speckling. There is also a "leadback" phase, which is very dark all over with possible light sprinkling.

Range Notes: The leadback phase is very rare or does not occur in Minnesota and Wisconsin. In Michigan, the leadback phase can be found on the Upper Peninsula only in the area of the Straits of Mackinac. In the North Woods of Lower Michigan, the lead-back phase represents about 10 percent of the population.

Adult on sphagnum moss showing the striking red back—its namesake. Inset: Eggs laid inside a rotting log.

Courtship, Mating & Eggs: During fall or spring, the male and female engage in courtship with the male rubbing his chin over the female's snout and the female straddling the male's tail and nudging the tail base. The male deposits a spermatophore, which the female takes into her cloaca. In June the female finds a small hollowed, moist place, such as inside or underneath a rotted log. She lays 3 to 17 eggs, which are often hung from above by a thin gelatinous stalk. The female guards the eggs for one to two months until they hatch. The little hatchlings have relatively big heads, plus tiny remnant gills that are soon absorbed; otherwise they look like the adults.

Nature Notes:

Secretive and hide during the day. On damp nights they emerge to search for invertebrates to eat, often climbing on the trunks of trees or other vegetation (see photo below).

Climbing the trunk of a Yellow Birch on a rainy night.

Order Anura – Frogs and Toads

Adult frogs and toads have a big head with no distinct neck, a short body with no tail and long muscular hind legs. Frogs and toads have big eyes with eyelids and a tympanum (for hearing) behind each eye. They have lungs for breathing, but oxygen can also be absorbed through the skin. Frogs and toads have long sticky tongues to help capture prey.

There are about 4,200 species of frogs and toads in the world, which are divided into about 26 families. Fourteen species in three families are found in the North Woods.

Family Bufonidae – True Toads

Over 400 species of toads in the world are in the family Bufonidae. Toads have thick, dry, warty skin that resists dehydration and produces irritating toxins. The glands producing the milky white poison are distributed across the toad's back, but are concentrated in the two parotoid glands on the back of the head. Toads have relatively short hind legs which are used for walking, hopping or burrowing by backing into the ground. Three species of toads inhabit the North Woods: the American Toad, Fowler's Toad and Canadian Toad.

Family Hylidae – Treefrogs

The family Hylidae has about 720 species worldwide. Treefrogs have toes with expanded adhesive discs called toe pads, which allows an arboreal life style. There are five species in the North Woods: Cope's Gray Treefrog, Gray Treefrog, Spring Peeper, Boreal Chorus Frog and the Western Chorus Frog.

Family Ranidae – True Frogs

Over 620 species of frogs in the world are grouped in the family Ranidae. These are the typical jumping frogs with long legs and webbed feet. They have large tympanums and most have dorsolateral ridges, which can be useful for identification. The North Woods are home to six species of these frogs: American Bullfrog, Green Frog, Pickerel Frog, Northern Leopard Frog, Wood Frog and Mink Frog.

Tadpole Comparison Chart

Gray Treefrogs

Tinged with red and spotted with black. Tail fin high, extending onto upper body.

Chorus Frogs

Brassy mottling. Tail fin clear or dark flecked. Tail musculature dark on top half.

Spring Peeper

Metallic gold flecks on back. Tail fin clear by musculature and blotched at outer edges. Musculature evenly blotched.

American Bullfrog

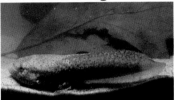

Green or brown with tiny dark spots above. Tail fin has round and distinct spots, mostly on top half.

Green Frog

Greenish body. Tail fin has evenly distributed speckles and dashes and is low on a muscular tail.

Pickerel Frog

Greenish or brownish. Both tail fin and tail musculature have large dark blotches.

Northern Leopard Frog

Green, olive or brown body. Tail fin light or clear, weakly spotted with black.

Wood Frog

Greenish to brown body often speckled with black and gold. Short high tail fin is light with small dark spots.

American Toad *Bufo americanus*

APRIL	MAY	JUNE	JULY	AUG	SEPT	OCT

Forests and open woodlands with moist soil for burrowing. Shallow ponds for breeding (flooded ditches to huge marshes).

Nature Notes:

Because it is terrestrial, it needs plenty of defenses. It has excellent camouflage in color and texture. It burrows into the ground or hides under logs. When threatened, it lowers its head, presenting its toxic parotoid glands to the predator. Further stressed, it secretes a milky white toxic substance from skin glands.

Meet the American Toad

Description: Length is 2 to 3½ inches.

The American Toad has the following features: cranial crests (ridges on top of head) that do not touch the parotoid glands (or only the tip touches), the largest dark spots contain only one or two large warts, the tibia (leg between thigh and foot) has enlarged warts and the chest is spotted. It can be gray, dark gray, brown, reddish brown or more, but will likely resemble an environmental constant like soil color.

Voice: A steady trill lasting about 30 seconds.

Courtship, Mating & Eggs: During late April or early May, American Toads migrate to shallow, temporary breeding ponds. Males arrive first, by as much as two weeks. The male calls from shallow water or shore. Any toad that happens by will be grabbed. If a male is

Males perch in shallow water so their vocal pouches will be out of the water when they give their mating call—a steady trill lasting up to 30 seconds. Inset: Thousands of eggs are laid in long pairs of gelatinous strings.

clasped by another male by mistake, he gives a one to five second release call trill while vibrating his sides. When he amplexes a female, enlarged thumbs help him maintain a tight grip if another male tries to dislodge him. The female swims to an egg laying site with the male hanging on her back. He fertilizes 2,000 to over 20,000 eggs as she lays them in a pair of long gelatinous strings.

Small black tadpoles hatch within two weeks. They metamorphose in 6 to 10 weeks.

Nature Notes:

When seized by a snake, which swallows prey whole, the toad inflates its body larger than the snake can swallow.

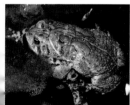

Male (on top) and female in amplexus. He will cling to her while she deposits the eggs.

A tiny toadlet moves onto land. Thousands may emerge from drying ponds.

A school of tadpoles may look like a single organism as they swim pond edges.

Fowler's Toad *Bufo fowleri*

APRIL	MAY	JUNE	JULY	AUG	SEPT	OCT

Open woodlands and open areas (avoids dense forests). Needs moist soil for burrowing and leaf litter and debris for hiding.

Nature Notes:

Fowler's Toad has all the defenses of the American Toad, but it might have one more. Reportedly it will sometimes play dead when roughly handled. Some predators will not feed on prey that is already dead.

Meet the Fowler's Toad

Description: Length is 2 to 3 inches.

Fowler's Toad can be distinguished from the American Toad in several ways. First of all, consider range: Fowler's Toad does not occur in Minnesota, Wisconsin or Michigan's Upper Peninsula. The parotoid glands of Fowler's Toad are up against the cranial crests, not just touching a tip. The largest black spots on the back contain three or more warts ↑. The tibia does not have greatly enlarged warts. The chest has no spots or perhaps one.

Voice: The male Fowler's Toad advertisement call, a low pitched nasal *"waaah,"* bears no resemblance to the American Toad's call.

Courtship, Mating & Eggs: Fowler's Toad uses a variety of temporary pools for breeding, which usually occurs later than the breeding of

Note that the largest black spots on a Fowler's Toad have three or more warts. American Toads only have one or two warts within a black spot.

American Toads in the same area. The female Fowler's Toad averages 7,000 to 10,000 eggs, deposited in two long strings. Inspection with a magnifying glass shows the egg-holding strings have no partitions, distinguishing them from the strings of American Toads where partitions keep eggs separate. The tiny black tadpoles, which look like American Toad tadpoles, hatch out in a few days and metamorphose about a month later.

Canadian Toad *Bufo hemiophrys*

APRIL	MAY	JUNE	JULY	AUG	SEPT	OCT

Woodlands and wetlands usually near a body of water.

Meet the Canadian Toad

Nature Notes:

Description: Length is 2 to 3 inches.

The Canadian Toad looks like an ordinary American Toad at first glance, but can be easily distinguished. First consider where it was found. Canadian Toads only enter the North Woods in northwestern Minnesota. Second, look at the top of its head. The Canadian Toad has a large boss or bump between its eyes ↑, formed by the merging of the cranial crests. The parotoid glands of the Canadian Toad are not well defined, blending into the skin around the edges.

Most Canadian Toads hibernate communally in mounds called Mima mounds. The mounds are believed to be formed by gophers and are composed of soil that is looser, allowing easier digging for toads. But a few toads hibernate individually in wooded uplands.

Voice: The advertisement call of the Canadian Toad is a low-pitched, weak trill lasting only two to five seconds.

Range Notes: The Canadian Toad has been found in Hubbard and Lake of the Woods

Canadian Toads can be distinguished from American Toads by the large bump between its eyes. It only enters the North Woods in north central and northwest Minnesota.

counties in Minnesota and farther west. It is not found elsewhere in the North Woods.

Courtship, Mating & Eggs: The eggs are laid in the shallows of ponds or lakes and hatch in a few days. The toadlets emerge from the water in late June or early July.

Nature Notes:

The Canadian Toad is more aquatic than other toads and will swim out into the water to escape danger.

Cope's Gray Treefrog *Hyla chrysoscelis*

APRIL	MAY	JUNE	JULY	AUG	SEPT	OCT

Woodland edges and more open country (Avoid deep forests).

Meet the Cope's Gray Treefrog

Nature Notes:

Description: Length is 1¼ to 1¾ inches.

Treefrogs are often seen feeding on insects attracted by lit windows and porch lights.

During the day, treefrogs hide in whatever nearby cavities are available, or they employ their protective camouflage and just hunker down on a leaf or against a tree trunk.

Cope's Gray Treefrog has slightly warty skin, slender legs and enlarged toe pads. Often a white, roughly square spot is under the eye and a dark band extends from the eye to the front leg. They can change color to gray or green or a mix in between. The groin and undersides of the rear legs are often washed with yellow or orange. Unfortunately, this description also fits the Gray Treefrog. In fact these two species were thought to be the same species until 1968. They are distinguished by their advertisement calls. Cope's is faster and shriller than the musical trill of the Gray. There are some visible differences that have emerged. Cope's Gray Treefrog has smoother skin. Often there is no pattern and the male tends to be all green when calling. If there is a pattern, Cope's Gray Treefrog has no black

Male Cope's photographed at night in a North Woods marsh. Best separated from Eastern Gray Treefrog by call. Cope's Gray Treefrog changes color for camouflage purposes but is often all green without blotching during the breeding season. Juvenile Cope's are mostly all green.

border around the blotches. Recently metamorphosed treefrogs of both species are bright green.

Voice: The call is a short, harsh trill.

Range Notes: Uncertain in some areas, since it was originally combined with that of the Gray Treefrog. Ranges sometimes overlap. Both species call from some of the same ponds.

Courtship, Mating & Eggs: About the middle of May, Cope's Gray Treefrogs begin calling from various small, ponds or the shallow edges of lakes. The males prefer perches just over the water and will defend territories. Satellite males lurk nearby to replace the resident male if he finds a female and leaves his perch. Females lay 1000 to 2000 eggs in small clusters attached near the surface. The eggs are hatched in a week and the tadpoles metamorphose six to eight weeks later.

Nature Notes:

Apparently Cope's Gray Treefrog never climbs more than ten feet high in a tree, because they are never heard calling from a higher perch.

The vocal sac helps create its short harsh trill.

Gray Treefrog *Hyla versicolor*

| APRIL | MAY | JUNE | JULY | AUG | SEPT | OCT |

Deciduous, coniferous and mixed forests. Unlike Cope's, often found in deep forests.

Nature Notes:

Sometimes a Gray Treefrog can be heard calling from high in a tree, before or well after breeding season. Some people mistake it for a bird. This is surely a Gray Treefrog because Cope's Gray Treefrog apparently doesn't call from over ten feet high.

Meet the Gray Treefrog

Description: Length is 1½ to 2 inches.

The Gray Treefrog can be gray or green, often with blotches. Usually adults have a roughly square white spot under the eye and a wash of yellow on the concealed surfaces of the back legs. Of course it looks very similar to Cope's Gray Treefrog. The two are best distinguished by their calls. The Gray Treefrog's call is a soothing, melodic trill as opposed to the harsher, faster, metallic trill of the Cope's. Other differences, though less reliable, include the Gray Treefrog having skin that's more warty and black edging around blotches. The tadpoles of both species have high tail fins tinged with red or orange and the newly meta-morphosed treefrogs are bright green.

Voice: Soft melodic trills.

Gray Treefrogs may be gray or green. Treefrog color is mostly a response to its environment, for camouflage, but humidity and temperature are also considered factors. The black edges of blotches remain, whether the frog is gray or green. Juveniles are mostly all green.

Courtship, Mating & Eggs: Gray Treefrogs breed in the middle of May, their soft melodic trills coming from ponds and marshes. The males call from the water or from perches on vegetation protruding from the water or hanging over it. Males hold territories about 30 inches from another male until they can attract a female and breed. Then a satellite male will likely take over the perch. The female lays 1000 to 2000 eggs as the male fertilizes them. The eggs are attached in small clusters to vegetation near the water's surface. Tadpoles hatch in three to seven days. The little bright green frogs leave the pond in six to eight weeks.

Top: A pair in amplexus.
Middle: Tadpole.
Bottom: Recently metamorphosed .

Western Chorus Frog *Pseudacris triseriata*

APRIL	MAY	JUNE	JULY	AUG	SEPT	OCT

Marshes, swamps and damp woods.

Nature Notes:

Chorus frogs are hard to find because of their small size and cryptic coloration.

They often call while hidden in grassy hummocks or other vegetation and usually go silent when approached.

After the breeding season, they are dispersed and rarely encountered.

Meet the Western Chorus Frog

Description: Length is ¾ to 1½ inches.

The Western Chorus Frog is tiny. The slightly bumpy skin is brown, tan, gray or olive, with three dark stripes down the back ↑. Occasionally the stripes break up posteriorly or are absent. A dark stripe runs through the eye and a white stripe runs along the upper lip. The toe pads are small. The hind legs appear normal in length as opposed to the short tibia of the Boreal Chorus Frog.

Voice: The Western Chorus Frog call is the rising *"crrreeek"* sound, similar to running a thumbnail along the teeth of a comb.

Courtship, Mating & Eggs: Chorus frogs are the first frogs to call in spring, usually beating spring peepers by a day or two. They cheat. They hibernate under logs or thick grasses close to the pond. Males call for about

The inflated vocal pouch acts as a resonator, amplifying the call. In general, the smaller the frog, the higher the pitch of the call.

a week before the females arrive. During amplexus the female lays 500 to 1,500 eggs, attaching elongated loose clusters to submerged plants. They hatch in 3 to 14 days and metamorphose 40 to 90 days after that.

This recently metamorphosed individual still has a remnant tail.

his is a darker individual.

Tadpole shows a brassy-colored mottling.

Boreal Chorus Frog *Pseudacris maculata*

| APRIL | MAY | JUNE | JULY | AUG | SEPT | **OCT** |

Marshy or boggy areas of boreal forests.

Nature Notes:

The Boreal Chorus Frog seems poorly equipped for survival. Its short tibia provides less leverage, reducing jumping ability to mere hops. The toe pads of chorus frogs are small, limiting climbing ability.

Meet the Boreal Chorus Frog

Description: Length is ¾ to 1½ inches.

The Boreal Chorus Frog until recently was considered a subspecies of the Western Chorus Frog. The Boreal Chorus Frog is often reddish brown or greenish and on the back are three green stripes that break into spots ↑. Sometimes it looks more spotted than striped. The best way to identify the Boreal Chorus Frog is to check a rear leg. The tibia (leg between thigh and foot) is very short ↑.

Voice: The call is very similar to the clicking *"crrreeek"* call of the Western Chorus Frog.

Courtship, Mating & Eggs: Boreal Chorus Frogs hibernate close to the pond to get the early jump on breeding. Eggs are laid in several loose clusters, hatch in a few days and the tadpoles may take two or three months to metamorphose.

The Boreal Chorus Frog often looks more spotted than striped (see Western Chorus Frog on page 62).

Spring Peeper *Pseudacris crucifer*

APRIL	MAY	JUNE	JULY	AUG	SEPT	OCT

Bogs, small ponds and other wetlands in deciduous and coniferous forests.

Meet the Spring Peeper

Nature Notes:

Spring Peepers overwinter hidden under leaf litter, logs or other material. They freeze, but glycerol in their body turns to glucose and acts as antifreeze. Its distribution protects organs and muscles, while allowing ice between them. With the spring thaw, the peepers also thaw for an early migration to the breeding pond.

Description: Length is ¾ to 1 inch.

The Spring Peeper is a treefrog with small toe pads. Its color can be tan, brown or gray, and usually has a characteristic dark X on its back ↑, although the X is often crooked or with extra lines (see middle photo on right hand page).

Voice: A whistling peep that slurs slightly up at the end.

Courtship, Mating & Eggs: Spring Peepers are among the earliest breeding frogs, calling from temporary ponds, bogs and other shallow wetlands in late March or early April. A male peeps about once per second. From a distance, a chorus of peepers sounds similar to sleigh bells. Spring Peeper males call from perches on vegetation sticking out of the water or along

Tadpole often flecked with metallic gold on the back. Inset: Close-up of developing tadpoles in eggs attached to submerged vegetation.

the shore and maintain territories. The Spring Peeper warning call is a stuttering "*creeek*" that sounds very similar to a chorus frog. Satellite males keep a low profile, looking to intercept a female or replace a successful resident male. The female lays 750 to 1,300 eggs, which are stuck to submerged vegetation singly or in small groups. The eggs hatch in a week or two and the tadpoles transform in 45 to 90 days.

The "X" on the back doesn't always look like an "X."

Tiny, newly metamorphosed Spring Peeper fits on a fingernail.

American Bullfrog *Rana catesbeiana*

APRIL	MAY	JUNE	JULY	AUG	SEPT	OCT

Permanent water with lots of vegetation, such as ponds, lakes, river sloughs or backwaters.

Nature Notes:

Often a bullfrog gives a warning call as it avoids danger by leaping into the water. A captured bullfrog may scream like a cat. The sudden shriek might startle a predator into dropping it. It might also attract a bigger predator to distract the first one.

Meet the American Bullfrog

Description: Length is 3¾ to 6 inches.

The largest frog in the North Woods. It has a ridge, the tympanic fold, which curves over and behind the tympanum ↑. It does not have dorsolateral ridges. The webbing of its foot does not reach the end of its longest toe. The male's tympanum is much larger than its eye, while the female's is about equal in size. The male's throat is yellow.

Voice: Its call is a bass toned, vibrating *"jug-o'-rum"* or *"rrrruuuummm"* that's loudest in the middle. The vocalization is produced as the internal vocal pouch swells the throat.

Courtship, Mating & Eggs: In the North Woods, American Bullfrogs breed during June and July. The male is territorial, sometimes having to win a shoving match to keep other

Note that the female's tympanum is the same size as her eye. Males would have a tympanum larger than the eye.

males 6 to 18 feet away. The female chooses the male and lays 5,000 to 20,000 black and white eggs during amplexus. The eggs float, black side up, in a thin sheet for 3 to 6 days until the tadpoles hatch. The tadpoles will overwinter once or twice, by hibernating in the bottom mud, before they metamorphose the following summer.

Nature Notes:

American Bullfrogs are voracious eaters that don't limit themselves to invertebrates. They have been known to eat fish, other frogs including bullfrogs, small turtles, birds and mammals.

Albinos lack all dark pigment—including the eyes.

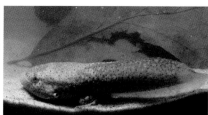

Note spiracle on side of head. This respiratory tube expels water after it has passed over the oxygen-hungry gills.

Green Frog *Rana clamitans*

APRIL	MAY	JUNE	JULY	AUG	SEPT	OCT

Shallow water and along the shores of most lakes and other permanent slow-moving or still bodies of water.

Nature Notes:

The Green Frog is the most commonly seen frog in the North. It often sits along the shore waiting for an insect snack.

Sensing danger, the Green Frog gives a squeaky warning cry while leaping into the water.

Meet the Green Frog

Description: Length is 2¾ to 3½ inches.

The Green Frog can be various shades of swamp green or brown with dark crossbands on the legs. A dorsolateral ridge extends at least half way down the body. The webbing of the hind foot is incomplete, with most of the longest toe free. The mature male has a yellow throat ↑, and its tympanum is larger than the eye ↑.

Voice: The male's advertisement call is an explosive *"gunk!"* like a loose banjo string. Often the call is instantly repeated with decreasing volume, resembling an echo. A warning call, like a louder single note advertisement call, is used to hold territory, but a physical battle is sometimes necessary.

Mature males show off beautiful yellow throats.

Courtship, Mating & Eggs: Green Frogs breed from late May into August. The female Green Frog chooses a male (or a good territory) and lays 3,000 to 4,000 floating eggs during amplexus. They hatch in 3 to 5 days. The tadpoles may overwinter before metamorphosing.

This Green Frog tadpole overwintered in the pond. It was photographed in spring.

See the Tadpole Comparison Chart on page 51 to differentiate frog tadpoles in our area.

Genus *Rana* TRUE FROGS | **71**

Pickerel Frog *Rana palustris*

| APRIL | MAY | JUNE | JULY | AUG | SEPT | OCT |

Grassy areas adjacent to clean, clear, cool water, such as trout streams, spring-fed bogs, fens and other wetlands.

Nature Notes:

Pickerel Frogs have toxic skin. Many predators that eat frogs, such as gartersnakes or water snakes usually won't touch the Pickerel Frog. Herons apparently recognize Pickerel Frogs and won't eat them.

Meet the Pickerel Frog

Description: Length is 1¾ to 3 inches.

The Pickerel Frog is tan or brown with two rows of roughly square darker brown spots down the back ↑, flanked by prominent dorso-lateral ridges. Spots elsewhere on the body and legs also appear roughly square or rectangular.

The groin and concealed surfaces of the hind legs are washed with bright yellow.

Voice: The male's call is a soft, one to two second snore, done while floating in the water or completely submerged.

Courtship, Mating & Eggs: Pickerel Frogs breed in April in the clear, cool, unpolluted waters they inhabit. The 800 to 3,000 eggs, brown above and yellow below, are attached in a loose clump to submerged vegetation.

Tadpoles are greenish or brownish and entire tail and fin covered with dark blotches.
Inset: A large clump of the Pickerel Frog's brown eggs attached to a submerged stick.

Tadpoles hatch in 10 to 21 days and metamorphose in two to three months.

Nature Notes:

Pickerel Frogs are devoured by Bullfrogs, Green Frogs and Mink (the mammal).

A Pickerel Frog's skin secretions may kill another frog (including another Pickerel Frog) if placed in the same collecting bag.

Recently metamorphosed frog still has its tail.

Northern Leopard Frog *Rana pipiens*

APRIL	MAY	JUNE	JULY	AUG	SEPT	OCT

Grassy areas near water. Lakes, are needed for hibernation.
Shallow ponds and backwaters are used for breeding.

Nature Notes:

The Northern Leopard Frog's preference of grassy areas for foraging often leads them to the large lawns of businesses. During dry weather, the frogs take advantage of automatic sprinklers for moisture, as they snap up the insects attracted by security lights.

Meet the Northern Leopard Frog

Description: Length is 2 to 3¾ inches.

The Northern Leopard Frog is green or brown with black spots. Dorsolateral ridges are prominent and extend to the groin.

Voice: The advertisement call is a low snore, which lasts several seconds and may be followed by some short clucks. The release call, given by males or unreceptive females, is a chuckling sound.

Courtship, Mating & Eggs: The Northern Leopard Frog breeds in early spring, although not as early as the Wood Frog, peepers or chorus frogs. Before the ice is gone from their lake or other large body of water, the Northern Leopard Frogs head out and migrate to marshes, ponds or backwaters to breed. These shallow waters are warmer. The male Northern

Northern Leopard Frogs have twin vocal pouches located above the front legs. Their call is a long snore.

Leopard Frog vocalizes while floating in the water or sometimes while submerged. During amplexus, the female lays 300 to 6,500 eggs that are black on top, white below and attached as an oval mass to submerged plants. Sometimes egg masses from many females are found in the same part of the pond.

Tadpole up close.

A mass of hundreds of eggs.

Mating takes place in April and May.

Mink Frog *Rana septentrionalis*

APRIL	MAY	JUNE	JULY	AUG	SEPT	OCT

Lakes in northern forests that have lots of floating or emergent vegetation. Sphagnum bogs bordering lakes.

Nature Notes:

As could be guessed by their fully webbed feet, Mink Frogs are more aquatic than other North Woods frogs. They habitually hang out in deeper water than other frogs and their diet includes a bigger percentage of aquatic invertebrates. When they do venture out onto a sphagnum mat, they're usually within jumping distance of the water.

Meet the Mink Frog

Description: Length is 1⅞ to 2¾ inches.

The Mink Frog looks similar to the Green Frog, but there are several differences. The Mink Frog has fully webbed feet, with webbing out to the last joint of the long toe and to the end of the outside toe. The Mink Frog is usually heavily mottled ↑ with dark spots or blotches, but more importantly, it has large dark spots, or sometimes lengthwise bars or stripes, on its hind legs. Green Frogs have some dark crossbands on the hind legs. Dorsolateral ridges vary from absent to prominent. If the Mink Frog's skin is scratched, it gives off an odor like a Mink or like rotten onions. The male has a tympanum larger than the eye and often a yellow throat.

Voice: The male's call, made while floating in the water or perched on a lily pad, is a rapid

Note the Mink Frog's large dark hindleg blotches. This is a good field mark to look for.

knocking "*cut cut cut cut.*" It sounds like distant hammering. A chorus sounds like galloping horses on a cobblestone street.

Courtship, Mating & Eggs: Mink Frogs usually breed in June and July. The female attaches 2,000 to 4,000 eggs to the stem of a plant, often deeper than three feet below the surface of the water. The tadpoles, because of the cold northern lakes and short growing season, may take one or two years to metamorphose.

Nature Notes:

Mink Frogs frequently sit on lily pads, sometimes distant from shore.

Mink Frogs prefer northern lakes with floating vegetation.

Note their fully webbed feet.

Wood Frog *Rana sylvatica*

APRIL	MAY	JUNE	JULY	AUG	SEPT	OCT

Woods; deciduous, coniferous or mixed. A closed canopy forest retains enough moisture for them. Only enters water for breeding.

Nature Notes:

The Wood Frog hibernates in the woods, under logs or leaf litter or loose soil. Here it is subjected to freezing temperatures, but survives by producing large amounts of glucose, which serves as an antifreeze. The organs and muscles are protected while allowing ice to form in spaces between them.

Meet the Wood Frog

Description: Length is 1⅜ to 2¼ inches.

The Wood Frog is recognized by its dark mask ↑. The Wood Frog can be tan or various shades of brown tinted with gray, red, pink or bronze. The dark brown mask starts at the snout, runs across most of the eye, covers the tympanum and ends above the front leg. It effectively hides the eye, which is very dark to match the stripe. A white stripe runs along the upper lip. The dorsolateral ridges may be accentuated by small black spots. Some Wood Frogs may have a white middorsal stripe.

Voice: A rapid-fired "*rack rack rack rack*," similar to a quacking duck.

Range Notes: Found farther north than any other North American amphibian. Even found in the Brooks Range of Alaska. The only amphibian found north of the Arctic Circle.

A smaller male mating with the larger female (amplexus). Inset: Wood Frog eggs in April.

Courtship, Mating & Eggs:
Wood Frogs are one of the earliest frogs to breed in spring, usually in a temporary woodland pond. The male floats on the surface while vocalizing. His thin vocal pouches, located over the front legs, expand with each *"rack."*

The female lays from 500 to over 3,000 eggs, which are attached just below the surface to submerged plant. The Wood Frogs disperse back into the woods after 6 to 14 days. The tadpoles hatch in four days to four weeks, depending on the highly variable temperatures of early spring.

Top: Calling male's vocal pouches are located above the front legs.
Middle: Tadpole has high tail fin lightly spotted.
Bottom: Newly metamorphosed frog.

Order Testudines – Turtles

The turtle is characterized by its protective shell. The bony structure of the shell is the rib cage, in which greatly expanded ribs and the vertebrae are fused together. Overlying the bone are horny shields called scutes or plates, although a few turtles just have a thick, leathery covering. The shoulders and hips have evolved to positions inside the rib cage. The top part of the shell is called the carapace, the bottom is the plastron, and they are connected on each side by the bridges. The plastron of some males, depending on species, is noticeably concave to fit over the female's carapace during copulation. Most turtles can withdraw the head and legs into the shell for protection. Those species with less armor due to a reduced plastron compensate with aggressive biting or speed. Really!

Another trait of turtles is having no teeth. They do have a sharp, horny beak covering the jaws. Turtles can't chew, but they bite into food and tear it to pieces with their clawed feet. Most turtles need to be submerged to swallow.

Turtles have sharp vision and most are wary.

Male turtles have a longer, thicker tail with the vent located farther out. The males of some species have long front claws.

All turtles are oviparous, laying shelled eggs, usually in a nest dug in the ground by the female. She covers the eggs and abandons them. Predators find most nests and eat the eggs. Those eggs that escape detection hatch in roughly 7 to 13 weeks, depending on species and incubation temperature.

That isn't all temperature affects. Some turtles have temperature-dependent sex determination. It seems strange, but there is a critical time during the middle third of incubation when the egg temperature determines the sex of the turtle. At higher temperatures, only females are produced. At lower temperatures, only males are produced (Painted Turtle, Northern Map Turtle, Blanding's Turtle, Spotted Turtle and Eastern Box Turtle). Two more species (Snapping Turtle and Stinkpot) fit this scenario, except that at still cooler temperatures they produce females again. Genetics seems to determine the sex ratios of Spiny Softshells and Wood Turtles, even though they don't have sex chromosomes like birds and mammals.

Cooler temperatures and shorter summers place limits on reproduction of North Woods turtles. Farther south many turtles nest twice a summer. Some North Woods Painted Turtles nest twice, but most, along with other turtle species, only nest once a season. It also takes more years for some species to reach maturity in the North Woods.

There are about 263 species of turtles worldwide, divided into about 13 families. The nine species of turtles in the North Woods represent four families.

Family Chelydridae – Snapping Turtles

Snapping turtles are brown or very dark, with a large head and long tail. The plastron is small, giving the legs mobility but not protection. Big sharp jaws and a nasty disposition compensate for the reduced plastron. One species, the Snapping Turtle is found in the North Woods.

Family Kinosternidae – Musk and Mud Turtles

Musk and mud turtles are small brown or black turtles with large heads and short tails. The elongated carapace is high and the plastron is small. A musky odor is emitted from glands on their sides where the skin meets the bridge. Musk and mud turtles are poor swimmers, preferring to walk on the bottom. Except for nesting, they don't often leave the water. When they are on land, they are aggressive biters. One species, the Stinkpot, inhabits waters of the North Woods.

Family Emydidae – Pond, Marsh and Box Turtles

This large family includes the typical aquatic turtles and also the terrestrial box turtles. The former are often seen basking on logs, ready to drop into the water if approached. Six species in six different genera are found in the North Woods: Painted Turtle, (Western and Midland subspecies), Spotted Turtle, Wood Turtle, Blanding's Turtle, Northern Map Turtle and Eastern Box Turtle.

Family Trionychidae – Softshells

Softshell turtles are highly aquatic and built for a submerged lifestyle, which explains their unique appearance. The flattened shell has a tough, leathery skin instead of horny scutes. The plastron is much reduced posteriorly, allowing free movement of the rear legs for swimming. The feet are large and fully webbed and not encumbered with scales. The neck is long and the nose is like a snorkel. One species, the Spiny Softshell, is found in North Woods waterways.

Snapping Turtle *Chelydra serpentina*

APRIL	MAY	JUNE	JULY	AUG	SEPT	OCT

Most permanent bodies of water, such as lakes, rivers, swamps or ponds. Mud bottoms and aquatic vegetation are preferred.

Nature Notes:

A large Snapping Turtle on land is a formidable sight. The reduced plastron allows it to walk with the body well off the ground. It drops down and turns with gaping jaws to face any threat. The snapper sometimes raises its posterior and lunges forward as it strikes out with its long neck.

Meet the Snapping Turtle

Description: Length is 8 to 14 inches.

The Snapping Turtle is the largest turtle in the North Woods with a carapace length up to 19¾ inches. The carapace scutes are raised and pointed at the rear, forming three keels. But the keels smooth out as the turtle ages. The plastron is small and cross-shaped, leaving the legs exposed from below. The snapper has a large head with big jaws, a long neck and a long tail. Males slightly larger than females.

Courtship, Mating & Eggs: A female Snapper might hike the better part of a mile to find a nesting site, or she might use the sloping bank of a stream. Over a hundred spherical white eggs might be laid (usually 25 to 50), which hatch in two to three months. Some stay in the nest over winter, but may freeze. It can be a long journey to water and some may

Snapping Turtles are usually only seen on land when the females travel to egg-laying sites in June. Note the ridged tail. Inset left: The tiny plastron is little protection. Fortunately, Snappers have few enemies and other formidable defenses. Inset right: A duckweed-covered adult assumes a defensive posture.

die from dehydration. Others will be eaten. Juvenile snappers are poor swimmers so some may drown.

In the North Woods, it may take a female 17 to 20 years to reach maturity.

Diet: A wide variety of invertebrates, small vertebrates and even plants. Studies have shown that Snappers are NOT a serious threat to waterfowl. In fact, the few ducklings lost to Snappers are insignificant compared to the raids of duck nests by mammalian predators.

Nature Notes:

In recent years Snapping Turtle numbers have declined, and the sizes of snappers harvested for food have also declined. Some regulations have been tightened.

Over 100 eggs may be laid in a nest excavated in soft soil.

Nests are raided by raccoons, fox, etc.

Hatchlings must still make the hazardous journey to water.

Stinkpot (Common Musk Turtle) *Sternotherus odoratus*

APRIL	MAY	JUNE	JULY	AUG	SEPT.	OCT

Shallow, clear water in lakes or slow-moving streams or back-waters.

Nature Notes:

Stinkpots are lousy swimmers and prefer to walk on the bottom in shallow water.

When still, they look more like rocks than turtles. Sometimes they bask out of water and have a reputation for climbing out on overhanging trees and dropping into a passing boat.

A Stinkpot lived 54 years in captivity.

Meet the Stinkpot

Description: Carapace length is 3 to 5 inches.

The Stinkpot—formerly called Common Musk Turtle—was named for its musky odor. This turtle has a domed, elongated carapace and a small plastron, offering little protection. The seam between the second and third sets of plastral scutes is hinged. Except for two yellow stripes on the side of its pointed head ↑, one above and one below the eye, the Stinkpot is drab brown to black. Its tail is short with a hardened nail at the tip. Hatchling Stinkpots are black with tiny white spots around the edge of the carapace and have the yellow head stripes. The carapace has at least a dorsal keel; sometimes two more.

Courtship, Mating & Eggs: The Stinkpot is the only North Woods turtle that might not

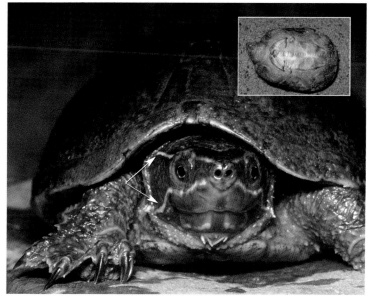

Note the adult Stinkpot's yellow-striped face and sturdy claws. Inset: Their plastron is small offering little protection.

bother digging a flask-shaped nest for the eggs. Sometimes the female lays the eggs, usually 3 to 5 and somewhat brittle, in a shallow excavation or under the edge of a log or bush. They might be half covered or not covered. Somehow enough survive to hatch in two to three months.

Diet: Worms, snails, aquatic insects, crayfish, tadpoles and fish. Also some carrion and plants.

Hatchlings are nearly black with small light spots around edge of carapace.

Turtle jaws are toothless but sharp.

Western Painted Turtle *Chrysemys picta bellii*

APRIL	MAY	JUNE	JULY	AUG	SEPT	OCT

Slow-moving streams, ponds, lakes and swamps with aquatic vegetation, muddy bottoms and basking sites.

Meet the Western Painted Turtle

Nature Notes:

Painted Turtles are the most common and most obvious turtle in the North Woods.

They're especially noticeable in the early spring when the sun is warm and the water is cold. In ponds where logs are few, turtles can be lined up or stacked on every available surface.

Description: Carapace length is 4 to 7 inches.

The Western Painted Turtle has a low, smooth, dark olive-green carapace with extensive red coloring on the plastron and ventral surface of the marginals. The upper jaw has a pair of sharp cusps flanking a notch. They have yellow stripes, but lack the red stripes on the legs and neck of the Midland Painted Turtle. The plastron has a larger dark pattern that extends out on some of the seams. Some have a dark reddish brown coating on the shell, most visible on the plastron. This is caused by the absorption of chemicals in the water. When the outer layer of the scutes is shed, so is the color. Males have long front claws and are smaller than females. The brightly colored hatchlings have a more circular carapace with a slight vertebral keel.

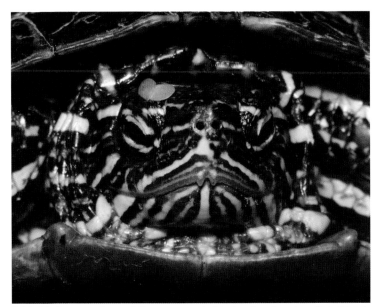

Painted Turtles are well named; they are very colorful when viewed up close. Note the pair of cusps on the upper jaw

Courtship, Mating & Eggs: Lays 3 to 20, usually 6 to 9, elliptical white eggs. The eggs hatch in 50 to 80 days but the young often overwinter in the nest. It takes females 6 to 10 years to reach maturity while males can breed in 3 to 7 years.

These eggs will hatch in 50 to 80 days.

Over 35 painted turtles vie for space on a prime basking log.

A colorful hatchling plastron.

Adult's plastron fades with age.

Hello world!

Midland Painted Turtle *Chrysemys picta marginata*

APRIL	MAY	JUNE	JULY	AUG	SEPT	OCT

Slow-moving streams, ponds, lakes and swamps with aquatic vegetation, muddy bottoms and basking sites.

Nature Notes:

Although Painted Turtles need to be submerged to eat, I've seen them crawl out of the water to snatch prey off the bank and return to the water to swallow it.

Because Painted Turtles are wide-ranging and abundant in many areas, they often serve as a child's introduction to reptiles.

Meet the Midland Painted Turtle

Description: Length is 4 to 6 inches.

The Midland Painted Turtle has yellow and red stripes ↑ on the forelegs and neck. The Midland Painted Turtle's plastron has the dark area concentrated in the middle.

Courtship, Mating & Eggs: Female lays 3 to 11 eggs. The biggest threat to Painted Turtles (including females searching out egg-laying sites) is traffic mortality as their habitat is intersected by more and more roads or completely hemmed in by development. In addition, the loss of large predators has resulted in an over-abundance of raccoons, skunks and other animals that search out turtle nests and devour the eggs.

Diet: Adult Painted Turtles (Western and Midland) are omnivorous, feeding on a variety

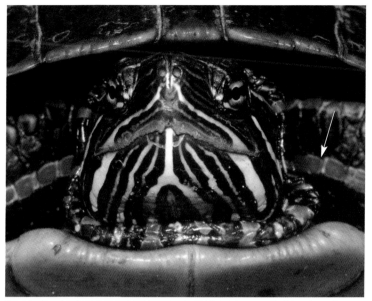

The adult's red-striped legs and red lower neck striping help separate this subspecies from the Western Painted Turtle.

of aquatic invertebrates and plants. Juveniles are more carnivorous and eat mostly insects, worms and tadpoles. The high protein diet contributes to rapid growth, which is critical for survival. As the turtle grows, it reduces the number of predators that can eat it.

Note how the dark area of the plastron is concentrated in the middle.

Compare this adult's plastron pattern to that of the Western Painted Turtle.

Hatchling Midlands don't acquire the red leg striping until older.

Genus *Chrysemys* PAINTED TURTLES

Spotted Turtle *Clemmys guttata*

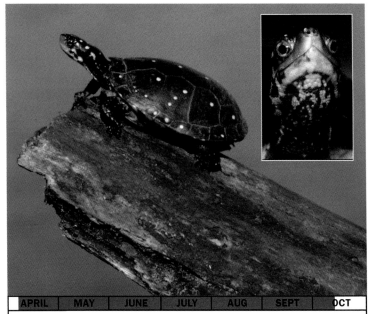

APRIL	MAY	JUNE	JULY	AUG	SEPT	OCT

Small ponds, shallow marshes, bogs and swamps. They need a mud bottom and vegetation.

Nature Notes:

In early spring, Spotted Turtles, especially males, move through deciduous woods and enter other ponds, including small vernal pools.

If disturbed while basking, they hide at the bottom under leaves or other debris.

A Spotted Turtle lived 42 years in captivity.

Meet the Spotted Turtle

Description: Carapace length is 3½ to 4½ inches.

The Spotted Turtle has a smooth black carapace sprinkled with yellow spots. The head is black with yellow or orange spots. The male has dark jaws and brown eyes, while the female has light jaws, a yellow or orange chin and orange eyes. The carapace of a hatchling Spotted Turtle usually has only a single spot.

Courtship, Mating & Eggs: In early spring, male Spotted Turtles will battle each other prior to courtship and mating with a female. In June the female digs a nest and lays 2 to 7 eggs, which hatch in 45 to 83 days. It takes a Spotted Turtle 7 to 14 years to reach breeding age.

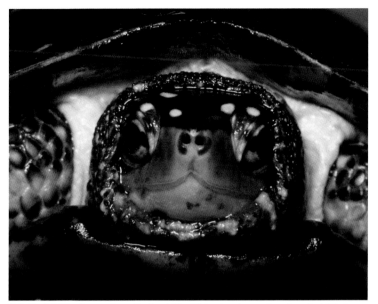

Note the bright yellow spots on the head. The light colored upper jaw show that this is a female

Diet: Prefers various aquatic invertebrates and tadpoles, but also eat aquatic vegetation.

Nature Notes:

During summer, Spotted Turtles are more secretive and may spend a lot of time just burrowed into the mud.

Plastron is distinctively marked.

Captive turtle eating a minnow.

Blanding's Turtle *Emydoidea blandingii*

APRIL	MAY	JUNE	JULY	AUG	SEPT	OCT

Shallow marshes, bogs, swamps and river backwaters. Aquatic vegetation and a muddy bottom are important.

Nature Notes:

A Minnesota specimen caught in 1989 was at least 77 years old!

Crayfish is their preferred food. It is stalked and seized with the jaws after a sudden thrust of the head and long neck. As the Blanding's Turtle strikes, the jaws open and the neck expands to suck in both water and prey. Various other invertebrates, tadpoles, frogs, fish and plants are eaten.

Meet the Blanding's Turtle

Description: Carapace length is 6 to 9 inches.

The Blanding's Turtle has a long neck with a bright yellow chin ↑ and throat that contrast sharply with the black or brown color of its shell, head and legs. The jaw is notched in front, giving the appearance of a smiling turtle. The smooth, domed carapace, which is shaped much like a helmet is sprinkled with yellow or tan. The plastron is yellowish with black patches at the outer rear of each scute. The plastron is hinged, allowing the two halves to be pulled against the carapace to protect the head and legs.

Courtship, Mating & Eggs: The male doesn't seem to have any elaborate courting behavior. He quickly swims over and against her carapace and bites at her head and neck until she allows him to mate with her.

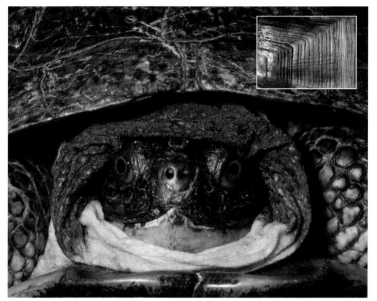

Blanding's have deeply notched upper jaw. Inset: Plastron detail showing growth annuli.

The female usually digs her nest in an open site with sandy soil and lays 6 to 21 elliptical eggs. They hatch in 50 to 75 days.

Blanding's basking (on right).

It takes 14 to 20 years to reach maturity. Studies of some populations have found that each year less than half of the adult females lay eggs. But as females age, they nest more often and have larger clutches of eggs. They seem not to decline physically and those over 50 years old are more productive than ever.

Female deposits eggs in sandy soil.

Diet: Crayfish, tadpoles, frogs, fish and plants.

Hatchling emerges.

Plastron has black patches on outer edges.

Wood Turtle *Glyptemys insculpta*

APRIL	MAY	JUNE	JULY	AUG	SEPT	OCT

At home in woods and water. Sandy-bottomed streams and rivers that flow through deciduous woodlands.

Nature Notes:

Wood Turtles have a unique method of finding worms. The turtle alternates stomping its front feet on the ground. Or the turtle lifts and drops the front of the plastron onto the ground. Possibly the sound or vibrations mimic raindrops, and the earthworm emerges to avoid drowning only to be gobbled up by the hungry Wood Turtle.

Meet the Wood Turtle

Description: Carapace length is 6 to 9 inches.

The Wood Turtle's carapace has the appearance of sculptured wood ↑. The scutes are brown, sometimes with radiating light or dark steaks, and each has concentric growth rings rising to form low pyramids. From these high points, tiny ridges radiate outward. The head is black, while the skin from the neck onto the legs is yellow or orange. The front legs have sturdy scales for better protection.

Courtship, Mating & Eggs: Both male and female extend their heads out towards each other, lower their heads and move them from side to side. Mating is usually in the water.

Likely nesting sites include high sand bars and sandy riverbanks and terraces. The female digs a flask-shaped hole and deposits 3 to 18 ellip-

Two hatchling Wood Turtles emerge from their nest along a river in northern Minnesota.
Inset: Captive Wood Turtle emerges from the egg.

tical eggs. She uses her back feet to fill the nest and often uses her plastron to smooth it over.

Diet: Worms, slugs, snails, berries, flower leaves.

Nature Notes:

At home on land and in the water, they often forage in the woods for food.

They don't wander more than a few hundred yards from their streams, but may range up to a mile along the banks.

In captivity a Wood Turtle lived 58 years.

Note yellow throat and upper legs.
Don't confuse with Blanding's Turtle.

The carapace appears sculpted.

Dark blotches are on rear outer edges.

Northern Map Turtle *Graptemys geographica*

| APRIL | MAY | JUNE | JULY | AUG | SEPT | OCT |

Rivers. They may also be found in backwaters, side channels, reservoirs and lakes. Fallen trees are favorite basking sites.

Meet the Northern Map Turtle

Nature Notes:

Northern Map Turtles are unusual in that males and females have significantly different diets. The female's large jaws have broad crushing surfaces adapted for crunching through the shells of clams, snails and crayfish.

Description: Carapace length of females average 7 to 10 inches. Males 4 to 6 inches.

The Northern Map Turtle has a brown or greenish gray carapace, often with dark blotches. There is a vertebral keel and the rear of the carapace is serrated ↑. Young individuals have light map-like lines on the carapace. The skin is greenish gray with thin yellow lines and an isolated yellow spot behind each eye ↑. The plastron is straw-colored. Females have a lower keel and a large broad head. The male has a smaller, narrower head and long front claws.

Range Notes: Found along the St. Croix River in Minnesota and Wisconsin, the Wolf River in Wisconsin and in western Lower Michigan.

Courtship, Mating & Eggs: The female lays 6 to 20 elliptical eggs during June or early

The Northern Map Turtle's upper jaw is curved. Also note the fine yellow and green striping on the neck.

July. They hatch in 50 to 70 days. Males are ready to breed in 3 to 5 years, but the larger females need 10 to 14 years to reach maturity.

Diet: All feeding done while submerged. Females eat river clams, snails and crayfish. Males feed on insects, small snails. Both will scavenge dead fish.

Eggs are laid in June or July.

Eggs hatch 50 to 70 days later.

Insects swarm around a sunning Map Turtle.

Hatchlings head for the water.

Eastern Box Turtle *Terrapene carolina*

APRIL	MAY	JUNE	JULY	AUG	SEPT	OCT

Deciduous or mixed forests, forest edges and semi-open areas near shallow water, such as bogs, marshes or small streams.

Meet the Eastern Box Turtle

Nature Notes:

Eastern Box Turtles are terrestrial. They forage on land for worms, slugs, snails, berries, etc.

Behavior is greatly influenced by weather. Slog around in boggy areas during hot days and, if heat and drought persist, will dig burrows and estivate (remain dormant) until conditions improve. They are most active during and after rain.

Description: Carapace length is 4½ to 6 inches.

The Eastern Box Turtle has a highly domed carapace. The plastron is hinged, allowing it to be pulled snug and tight against the carapace when the turtle needs protection. Shell color varies tremendously. It can be brown or very dark with yellow or orange streaks, but the yellow or orange can also be the dominant color. Usually the male has red eyes ↑ and the female has brown eyes.

Courtship, Mating & Eggs: Mating seems an impressive accomplishment for a male box turtle. When mounting the female from behind, he has to overcome the female's high domed carapace, and the fact that both male and female have short tails. But the posterior third of the male's plastron is concave, and he hangs onto the female's carapace with the

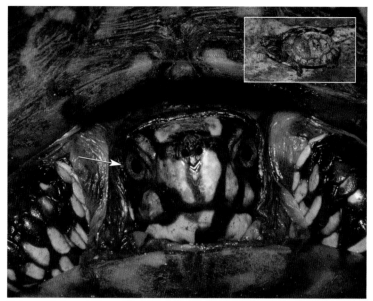

Males usually have striking red eyes. Inset: Juvenile showing flatter shell with vertebral ridge.

curved claws of his rear legs. The male's plastron is vertical while mating. Afterwards, the male often tips over backwards, risking death if he cannot right himself.

A beautifully-marked male is on the move during a rainy afternoon.

The female selects a nesting site, usually an area open to the sun, and deposits 3 to 11 eggs. The eggs hatch in 2 to 3 months and the young may overwinter in the nest. Box turtles in the North need about 10 years to reach maturity.

Worms are a favorite food.

A park ranger recently discovered an Eastern Box Turtle with a date and initials carved in the plastron. He learned that a previous naturalist, had marked nearly a thousand box turtles back in the 1930s. These turtles are certainly old, but the longevity record is 138 years!

Diet: Worms, slugs, snails, berries, etc.

A hinged plastron allows for full closure.

Spiny Softshell *Apalone spinifera*

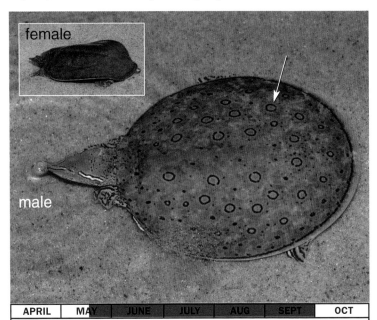

| APRIL | MAY | JUNE | JULY | AUG | SEPT | OCT |

Rivers with a sandy bottom and sandy banks. Will also inhabit lakes and waters with muddy bottoms.

Nature Notes:

The softshell is highly adapted to water; webbed feet and streamlined shape allow fast swimming.

Oxygen absorbed through the throat, cloaca and skin to help the turtle remain submerged for long periods of time.

Buried in a sandy bottom, its long neck and snorkel-like nose can reach the water's surface.

Meet the Spiny Softshell

Description: Carapace length of females averages 7 to 18 inches. Males 5 to 9½ inches.

The Spiny Softshell bears a definite resemblance to a large pancake. Its shell is round, flattened and lacks horny scutes. The edges are flexible. The feet are large and strongly webbed. The softshell's neck is long and its nose is long and tubular ↑. Two black-bordered yellow stripes, one behind the eye and one behind the mouth. Adult males have small spots and circles ↑ called ocelli and the carapace feels gritty like sandpaper. Adult females are larger with a blotchy camouflage pattern. At the front edge of the female's carapace are sharp, spiny projections.

Courtship, Mating & Eggs: Softshell claws are sharp and the shell is vulnerable so the male hovers over the female during mating.

The snorkel-like nose helps reach the surface while the turtle remains hidden. Inset left: Note the C-shaped nostrils that separate this species from its more southerly cousin—the Smooth Softshell. Inset right: Softshells will often bury themselves in sandy bottoms.

Softshells will nest as close to the water as possible. She selects a site on a raised sandbar or on the slope of a riverbank to lay her eggs. She quickly digs a hole and deposits 9 to 38 spherical white eggs. The eggs hatch in 55 to 85 days.

Males reach maturity in 4 to 5 years, while the larger female requires 8 to 10 years.

Diet: Prefers crayfish and other aquatic invertebrates but would not turn up its pointy nose at a tadpole or fish.

Nature Notes:

In early spring, softshells frequently bask. When sunning on a riverbank, the turtle faces the water for a quick escape.

The softshell is actually speedy on land.

Minnesota's state record Spiny (carapace 19 1/4 inches) was estimated to be 60 to 70 years old when it was captured and released.

Hatchlings have a tubular nose too.

Basking on a river log. Note the large hind feet.

Order Squamata
Lizards and Snakes

Lizards and snakes are covered with scaly skin that protects the body and retains moisture. Some lizards and snakes have smooth scales and others have keeled scales. A keeled scale has a central ridge running its length and the overall effect is that the reptile has a rough appearance. Smooth scales make an animal look shiny. The type of scale a lizard or snake has is important in identification. The outer layer of skin is periodically replaced as the animal grows.

The tongue is used for sensory purposes as it flicks out and picks up minute particles from the air. Some lizards have a long forked tongue like a snake, while most have a shorter, blunt-tipped tongue. The tongue tips contact Jacobson's organ, located on the roof of the mouth. The sense, similar to the sense of smell, is called chemoreception and is useful in detection of food, enemies or the opposite sex.

Male lizards and snakes have a double penis called hemipenes. Only one is used during mating.

Suborder Sauria – Lizards

Even though a few lizards are legless, they differ from snakes in several ways. Most lizards have eyelids while snakes never do. Lizards have ear openings and snakes don't. The lower jaw bones of lizards are fused, so they can't stretch apart to accommodate large prey. Lizards do not have the broad ventral (belly) scales that snakes can use for crawling. Some lizards can break off the tail to escape a predator and grow a new one.

About 4,450 species of lizards in 22 families are known worldwide. Two species in a single family occur in the North Woods.

Family Scincidae – Skinks

Most skinks are designed for escape. Often a fast moving skink doesn't use its small legs, instead folding them back and using a rapid snake-like swimming motion. If the tail is grabbed, it promptly breaks off, leaving the predator with a wiggling distraction. The skink's tail will regenerate, though it will be dull colored with no pattern. If the skink is caught, its streamlined shape and smooth, shiny scales, make the squirming lizard slick and difficult to hold.

The Five-lined Skink and the Prairie Skink are found in parts of the North Woods.

Suborder Serpentes – Snakes

Snakes have no legs, no eyelids and no ear openings. The eye is protected by a clear scale called the brille. The lower jaw bones are not fused together but are connected by stretchable ligaments, allowing the jaws to engulf large prey. The jaws alternate as each side reaches forward and pulls the prey a little farther into the mouth. Tiny backward-curved teeth help maintain a grip on the animal.

Snakes move by lateral undulation, which is the side to side motion used for swimming, or crawling fast through bushes or on the ground. The snake pushes off from S-shaped loops of the body. Snakes can slowly crawl straight ahead by rectilinear locomotion, using the broad belly scales or ventral scutes, as each scale edge pushes against the ground, shifts forward and pushes again. Some scales are doing the gripping and pushing while others are sliding ahead. This technique works well enough that some snakes can use it to crawl up a tree trunk

Prior to shedding, lymphatic fluid moves between the new skin and the outer layer. The eyes turn blue but then clear just before shedding. The snake rubs its nose and mouth against objects to start pulling the skin off. The snake crawls out of the skin as it peels back and is left inside out.

To eat, some snakes simply seize the prey in their jaws and overpower it. Tiny, sharp teeth curve backwards, helping to secure the animal. Some snakes grasp the prey, wrap coils around it and constrict tight enough to stop the animal's heart or breathing. A rattlesnake injects venom as it strikes the prey and then avoids further risk by letting the animal wander off to die. The venom starts the digestive process. The rattlesnake locates the animal by following its scent and swallows it head first.

Family Colubridae – Typical Snakes

The family Colubridae is a huge conglomeration of harmless snakes, containing about 1,560 species throughout the world. In North America, any snake that isn't a blind snake, boa, sea snake, coral snake or pit viper was dumped into this family. Colubrids are a diverse group of snakes. Some have rear fangs with mildly toxic saliva, some constrict their prey and some lay eggs while others bear live young. Many of these harmless snakes imitate rattlesnakes by vibrating their tails, which often makes a buzzing sound against dry leaves or brush. Colubridae is already divided into subfamilies. In the future one or more of these could be elevated to the family level.

The North Woods is home to 13 species of these so-called typical snakes.

Family Crotalidae – Pit Vipers

The Copperhead, Cottonmouth and rattlesnakes are all pit vipers, named for the heat-sensitive pit located between each eye and nostril. The pits detect heat as infrared radiation and allow the snake to accurately strike a mouse in complete darkness. Another nocturnal adaptation is elliptical pupils.

Pit vipers are venomous snakes with a pair of large hollow fangs that fold back against the roof of the mouth when not in use. The fangs are connected by ducts to the venom glands, which are modified saliva glands at the rear of the head. The size of the venom glands gives the pit viper its characteristic triangular-shaped head. When the snake strikes, the mouth opens wide and the fangs rotate out, so they point forward. As the fangs stab into the target, muscles contract to force venom out through the fangs. The snake controls the amount of venom injected. It may not inject any venom if the strike is defensive.

One pit viper, the Massasauga, inhabits the North Woods.

Common Five-lined Skink *Eumeces fasciatus*

juvenile

adult male

APRIL	MAY	JUNE	JULY	AUG	SEPT	OCT

Damp sandy soil with logs or rocks for basking. Forest edges, oak or pine barrens, rock outcrops, beaches with driftwood.

Nature Notes:

Common Five-lined Skinks become active in late April or early May.

When threatened, the skink may run up the trunk of a tree, but more likely it will tuck its small legs along its sides and rapidly wiggle snake-like into the grass or under cover. It may also dash into its burrow, which it previously dug in the sandy soil.

Meet the Five-lined Skink

Description: Length is 5 to 8½ inches including tail. Maximum snout-vent length (since the tail may be lost or shorter due to regeneration) is 3⅛ inches long.

The Common Five-lined Skink is a smooth shiny lizard with small legs. Color varies but is most brilliant in juveniles. A juvenile Five-lined Skink has five thin white or yellow stripes against a black background, with the dorsal stripe splitting into a "Y" on the head. The tail is bright metallic blue ↑. A young adult female maintains the pattern and most of the color. Older females look faded with tan stripes on a brown background and a blue-gray tail. Adult males are brown with faint stripes and a gray tail. Males have orange jaws ↑, which become reddish orange during the breeding season.

female

Female skinks guard their eggs until they hatch. When the tiny blue-tailed young emerge they quickly disperse.

Courtship, Mating & Eggs: The male defends territory, allowing the presence of blue-tailed juveniles and females but chasing away orange-faced males. About a month after breeding, the female lays 5 to 18 eggs in a moist, hidden place. She tends the eggs and guards them until they hatch and the young disperse.

Skinks mature in the second or third year.

Diet: Many invertebrates. Occasionally a large skink will eat a baby mouse or tiny frog.

Nature Notes:

If grabbed by the tail, the skink can break it off, leaving the predator with a wiggling distraction (see photo below). The skink grows a new tail, which will be a dull gray and never as long.

Typical Five-lined Skink habitat.

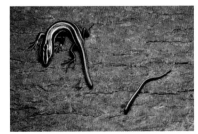

A new but shorter tail will regenerate.

Prairie Skink *Eumeces septentrionalis*

APRIL	MAY	JUNE	JULY	AUG	SEPT	OCT

Sandy soil habitats; pine barrens, stream banks, road cuts or grassy areas. Also rock outcrops, gravelly glacial outwashes.

Nature Notes:

Prairie Skinks dig burrows in sandy soil where they spend the night, and even the day, if the weather doesn't appeal to them. When they do come out, they bask in the sun and hunt invertebrates.

When threatened, they hold their small legs back against their bodies and use a rapid serpentine motion to wiggle through the grass.

Meet the Prairie Skink

Description: Length is 5¼ to 8¾ inches including tail. The maximum snout-vent length is 3½ inches.

The Prairie Skink is a smooth shiny lizard with small legs. Juveniles have seven light stripes and bright blue tails. The adult Prairie Skink is gray to light brown with stripes. The most prominent stripe is a thin white or light dorso-lateral stripe ↑ bordered by wider black or very dark brown stripes. The skink's back has two dark stripes which can be either distinct or muted. Adult males develop orange faces during the breeding season.

Courtship, Mating & Eggs: In late June or early July, the female Prairie Skink hollows out a nesting site and lays 5 to 13 eggs. She tends the eggs and guards them until they hatch in

This Prairie Skink's orange face means that this is a male. During the breeding season the orange becomes even brighter.

40 to 52 days. She will stay and guard the young for two or three days until they disperse. The young are ready to breed during their second spring.

Diet: Prairie Skinks feed on crickets, beetles, caterpillars, other insects and spiders.

Nature Notes:

The tail is detached easily if grabbed. It will regenerate and be shorter and plain looking.

Only juveniles have a blue tail.

A cricket becomes a meal for a Prairie Skink.

Eastern Racer *Coluber constrictor*

adult

APRIL	MAY	JUNE	JULY	AUG	SEPT	OCT

Dry sunny areas such as hillsides, forest edges, open woods and grasslands.

Nature Notes:

Eastern Racers are diurnal, alert, fast snakes that crawl with the head and neck elevated to better spot the movement of potential prey.

They use their speed to catch frogs, snakes or mice. Bird eggs or young are also on the menu, and the Eastern Racer will climb through bushes to get them.

Meet the Eastern Racer

Description: Length is 3 to 6 feet.

The Eastern Racer in the North Woods is bluish gray with large eyes. The chin and throat are white or yellowish and the belly pale blue. The scales are smooth. Juvenile Eastern Racers look nothing like the adult coloration. The juveniles are heavily blotched with dark reddish brown on a gray or tan ground color. The head and belly are spotted. Attaining the adult coloration takes a year or two.

Range Notes: The Eastern Racer is found on the western side of Lower Michigan and an isolated population occurs in Menominee County in Upper Michigan. In Minnesota the Eastern Racer enters the North Woods in Pine County.

Courtship, Mating & Eggs: The male Eastern Racer will follow the pheromone trail of a female and catch up to her. His body rip-

juvenile

Juveniles are blotched with dark spots and look nothing like the adults. This stage lasts a year or two.

ples with movement as they entwine and mate. In late June or July she lays 3 to 32, usually 8 to 20 elongated oval eggs with a granular texture. They hatch in August or early September. Males take one or two years to mature while females require two or three.

Diet: Frogs, lizards, snakes, mice, bird eggs and young birds.

Nature Notes:

Contrary to their Latin species name, they do not constrict prey but simply overpower it.

Speed is used to escape enemies, but when cornered the racer will coil defensively, vibrate its tail and bite.

Juvenile beginning to shed its skin.

The hatching process begins.

Western Foxsnake *Elaphe vulpina*

| APRIL | MAY | JUNE | JULY | AUG | SEPT | OCT |

Forest edges, bottomland forest, pine barrens, old fields, marshes and railroad beds through wetlands. Always near water.

Meet the Western Foxsnake

Nature Notes:

Some people mistake the Western Foxsnake for venomous species because it vibrates its tail and has blotches instead of stripes. Many foxsnakes have been killed because of this ignorance. Fortunately, many escape notice because their coloration and pattern provides excellent camouflage.

Description: Length is 3 to 4½ feet long. Record length of 5 feet 10½ inches.

The adult's head is orange-brown ↑, brown or grayish brown. Large brown saddle-like blotches run down the back, with alternating smaller blotches on the sides. The ground color is yellowish brown or grayish brown. Scales are keeled dorsally but are smooth on the sides. The ventral scutes are yellowish with small dark squares.

Juveniles are gray with dark blotches. The head is marked with a dark line connecting the eyes and another line extends from each eye to the angle of the jaw.

Courtship, Mating & Eggs: Males combat each other for dominance by trying to raise up high enough to push over and pin his opponent to the ground. A male moving beside a

A White-footed Mouse goes down head first. Small rodents are a major part of their diet.

female will adopt a jerking motion. She might move in the same way. The male usually takes hold of her neck or head with his mouth. They intertwine bodies and mate.

In July, the female lays 7 to 27 eggs, which adhere to each other. They hatch in late August or early September.

Diet: Kill by constriction. Mainly mice and voles. Squared ventral scutes help them climb trees for birds and bird eggs. Juveniles eat worms, frogs and small reptiles.

Nature Notes:

Hibernate by migrating to a hillside hibernaculum or old foundation. Surprisingly, they also hibernate submerged in old wells.

Foxsnakes have a musky odor similar to a Red Fox.

The defensive coil is a scare tactic.

Foxsnakes often hunt along railroad right-of-ways.

Milksnake *Lampropeltis triangulum*

APRIL	MAY	JUNE	JULY	AUG	SEPT	OCT

Rocky hillsides, in bottomland woods, open woods or fields. Cover, such as flat rocks, is important.

Nature Notes:

Milksnakes are more common than most people realize because of their secretive habits. They hide under flat rocks, boards, tin or in burrows.

Milksnakes are mostly nocturnal, especially in the summer. When they are out during daylight hours, they have very effective cryptic coloration.

Meet the Milksnake

Description: Length is 24 to 36 inches. Record length of 52 inches.

The Milksnake's head is reddish brown or brown with usually a light Y- or V-shaped blotch on the nape.

The Milksnake has smooth scales with large saddle-like reddish brown dorsal blotches. Alternating with them are smaller blotches on the sides. The ground color is gray or tan. The belly is white, checkered with black. Juveniles are light gray with bright red blotches.

Courtship, Mating & Eggs: Milksnakes mate when they emerge from hibernation or later in the spring. In late June or early July, the female lays 5 to 24 eggs, which usually stick together in a clump. After 6 to 9 weeks the eggs hatch. Milksnakes mature in their third or fourth year.

The round pupil and lack of a facial pit indicates that it's a harmless snake. Inset: Cryptic coloration helps make Milksnakes virtually disappear on lichen-covered rocks.

Diet: Kill by constriction. They feed on mice, voles, birds, bird eggs, snakes and lizards.

Nature Notes:

When threatened, Milksnakes will coil and vibrate their tails, producing a buzzing noise in dry leaves or brush.

Milksnake eggs adhere together in a clump.

Egg is slit by young's egg tooth.

Genus *Lampropeltis* KINGSNAKES

Smooth Greensnake *Opheodrys vernalis*

APRIL	MAY	JUNE	JULY	AUG	SEPT	OCT

Moist grassy areas associated with lakes, marshes, bogs and meadows. Also open woods and oak savannas.

Nature Notes:

Smooth Greensnakes are well camouflaged as they move through grass and the leaves of low bushes. When not foraging, they are usually hiding underneath something, such as a flat rock or log.

Unfortunately, these harmless, beneficial snakes have been adversely affected by the widespread use of pesticides.

Meet the Smooth Greensnake

Description: Length is 12 to 20 inches. Record length of 26 inches.

The Smooth Greensnake has smooth leaf-green scales with a white or pale yellow underside. The Smooth Greensnake is unmistakable, except when it's a different color. Instead of green, some are actually tan or rarely, bronze. Hatchlings can be dark green, bluish gray or brown. Whatever the color, the smooth scales and lack of pattern distinguish this species from the Brownsnake. Death causes a green snake to turn blue. But a similar sized Blue Racer would still have juvenile spotting.

Courtship, Mating & Eggs: Smooth Greensnakes usually breed in spring but egg-laying may extend into September. The female selects a moist, hidden site, such as inside or underneath a rotting log. Sometimes more

Not all Smooth Greensnakes are green but they all have smooth scales. This is the brown morph. Rarely they may be bronze colored.

than one female chooses the same nesting location. The eggs hatch in only 4 to 30 days. The young probably reach breeding size in their second year.

Diet: Feed primarily on insects, such as crickets, grasshoppers, beetles and hairless caterpillars.

Nature Notes:

Sometimes many Smooth Greensnakes hibernate together with other small snakes in abandoned ant mounds.

Hatchling Smooth Greensnakes may be dark green, bluish gray or brown.

A threatening pose from a harmless snake.

Ring-necked Snake *Diadophis punctatus*

| APRIL | MAY | JUNE | JULY | AUG | SEPT | OCT |

Moist, shaded forests or forest edges but not river bottom forests.

Meet the Ring-necked Snake

Nature Notes:

Ring-necked Snakes aren't often seen because they are secretive, hiding under logs or rocks by day. They come out at night to forage for small prey.

Eastern Red-backed Salamanders are a frequent food item.

Description: Length is 10 to 15 inches. Record length of $27^{11}/_{16}$ inches.

The Ring-necked Snake is bluish black or bluish gray or brownish, with a bright orange or yellow collar ↑. The scales are smooth and shiny. The belly is yellow or orange-yellow. Juveniles are similarly colored but darker.

Courtship, Mating & Eggs: Mating can take place from spring through fall. The female can store sperm until spring, if that's when she lays the eggs. The 1 to 10 eggs are noticeably elongated and frequently have tapered ends. Often the eggs are placed in the same moist, hidden site selected by others females. Most eggs hatch in the second half of August or early September. Maturity isn't attained until the second or third year.

A close up showing the distinctive ring around the neck.

Diet: Worms, small snakes, lizards, frogs and salamanders.

Nature Notes:

Ring-necked Snakes have saliva that may be slightly toxic.

Ring-necked snakes are usually colonial, with many inhabiting a small local area.

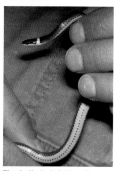

The belly is bright yellow with black spots.

Eastern Hog-nosed Snake *Heterodon platirhinos*

| APRIL | MAY | JUNE | JULY | AUG | SEPT | OCT |

Sandy soil habitats such as sand prairies, oak savannas and open pine or deciduous woods.

Nature Notes:

The Eastern Hog-nosed Snake is well known for its acting ability. When threatened, or even merely approached, the snake often launches into a dramatic threat display. It flattens its body and spreads out its neck like a cobra (see main photo this page). It coils and gapes its mouth while hissing loudly. It may strike with its mouth closed.

Meet the Eastern Hog-nosed Snake

Description: Length is 20 to 33 inches. Record length of 45½ inches.

The Eastern Hog-nosed Snake is a stocky snake that has a upwardly curved rostral scale forming its characteristic upturned nose. Scales are keeled. Most hog-nosed snakes have large blotches down the back alternating with smaller blotches on the sides. Color is highly variable; may be yellow, black, gray, brown, reddish brown, tan, olive. Most have a pair of large black spots behind the head that resemble large eyes when they flatten their neck defensively. Color may reflect habitat. Tan colored snakes match sandy soil. Dark brown snakes inhabit wooded areas. Juveniles are distinctly patterned and have a dark line connecting the eyes and one from eye to jaw.

Courtship, Mating & Eggs: Lay 4 to 61 eggs, which are wider than most snake eggs. They

Hog-nosed Snakes are great actors; this one is playing dead to deter predators. But put him back on his belly and he will writhe around and flip back over! Inset: Typical sandy habitat.

hatch in about two months. Hatchlings can immediately perform their bluffing and death acts. Adulthood in the second or third year.

Diet: Their upturned nose is for digging up burrowed toads. The toad's skin toxins deters most predators, but they don't bother the hog-nosed snake. The toad inflates its body, trying to prevent being swallowed whole, but a pair of enlarged, upper rear teeth puncture the doomed toad. Will also eat frogs, salamanders, small reptiles, birds, small mammals.

Nature Notes:
(continued)

If this bluffing fails to scare away the perceived threat and the hognose is gently poked a couple times, it changes tactics. The hog-nose starts writhing and twisting. Its tongue hangs out. It may empty its cloaca of stinking wastes and musk. It rolls onto its back and lies still with its tongue still hanging out. It looks and smells dead.

Hatchlings can bluff and play dead just like the adults.

The "cobra act" displays black "eyes."

Toads are a favorite food. Mildly toxic saliva may help subdue prey.

DeKay's Brownsnake *Storeria dekayi*

| APRIL | MAY | JUNE | JULY | AUG | SEPT | OCT |

Bogs, swamps, marshes, moist woods and wooded hillsides.

Meet the DeKay's Brownsnake

Nature Notes:

DeKay's Brownsnakes feed on slugs, earthworms, soft-bodied insects and insect larva. They also feed on snails by employing specialized jaws and teeth to pull the soft body from the shell.

They are normally secretive, hiding by day and coming out at night to feed.

Description: Length is 9 to 13 inches. Record length of 20¾ inches was for a Midland Brownsnake.

The DeKay's Brownsnake's scales are keeled, with 17 rows at midbody. They are brown, dark brown, reddish brown or grayish brown. The middle of the back is usually lighter in color and bordered by small dark spots. Some spots opposite each other are linked with a dark line. The belly is buff, cream-colored or pinkish. Some brownsnakes have one or two dark marks below each eye and some have dark blotches on each side of the neck. These types of markings are largely inconsistent for distinguishing subspecies. Juvenile DeKay's Brownsnakes are similarly colored but have light patches behind the head, which are sometimes connected, forming a collar.

Every spring brownsnakes migrate from hibernaculums to their summer habitat.

Range Notes: The Brownsnake is found throughout Lower Michigan (Midland X Northern subspecies), northeast Wisconsin and isolated parts of Upper Michigan (Midland subspecies) and northwestern Wisconsin plus the North Woods boundary in Minnesota (Texas subspecies).

Courtship, Mating & Young: After mating in the spring, the female gives birth to 3 to 41 young (no eggs), usually about a dozen, and usually in late July or August. There is no maternal care, although they may be found together for a few days.

Diet: Slugs, worms, soft-bodied insects, insect larva and snails.

Nature Notes:

Brownsnakes are most often seen on country roads during their fall migration from moist bottomlands to wooded hillsides where they will hibernate. They also make a spring migration.

Brownsnakes bear live young.

Red-bellied Snake *Storeria occipitomaculata*

| APRIL | MAY | JUNE | JULY | AUG | SEPT | OCT |

Boreal forests, hardwood forests, open woods, sphagnum bogs and marshes.

Meet the Red-bellied Snake

Nature Notes:

Red-bellied Snakes feed on snails by extracting them from their shells with teeth and jaws specialized for that purpose. They also eat slugs, earthworms and other small, soft-bodied creatures.

Description: Length is 8 to 10 inches long, with a record length of 16 inches.

The Red-bellied Snake has keeled scales with 15 scale rows at midbody. They have two basic color phases: gray or reddish brown. Rarely, a black one is found. They may have a lighter dorsum like the DeKay's Brownsnake, but they lack the rows of spots and usually have two or four thin black stripes. The belly is bright red ↑; usually. Red-bellied Snakes have been found with ventral colors of orange, light yellow, pink or even gray or bluish black. Red-bellied Snakes have three tan or yellowish spots behind the head: one on the nape and one on each side of the neck. These spots may be merged into a collar. The Red-bellied Snake also has on the fifth upper labial, a distinctive light mark with black underneath. Minnesota

This is the reddish-brown phase of the Red-bellied Snake. They can also be dark gray.

specimens may lack the neck spots and labial mark because of the influence of the Black Hills Red-bellied Snake subspecies.

Range Notes: The intergrade of the Northern and Black Hills Red-bellied Snake subspecies is found in Minnesota.

Courtship, Mating & Young: Some time during late July, August or early September, a mated female Red-bellied Snake will give birth to 1 to 21 young, with seven or eight being a common number.

Diet: Snails, slugs, earthworms and other invertebrates.

Nature Notes:

Red-bellied Snakes migrate to hibernaculums, such as abandoned ant mounds, where they hibernate with other small snakes.

The red ventral scales create the red belly it's named for.

Northern Watersnake *Nerodia sipedon*

APRIL	MAY	JUNE	JULY	AUG	SEPT	OCT

Permanent bodies of water, including rivers, sloughs, lakes, marshes, bogs or ponds with logs or open banks for basking.

Meet the Northern Watersnake

Nature Notes:

Northern Watersnakes feed mostly on cold-blooded vertebrates, such as fish, frogs, tadpoles or salamanders. They have no impact on game fish. Prey is hunted on land or in the water and smaller prey can be swallowed while submerged.

Description: Length is 24 to 36 inches. Record length of 4 feet 7½ inches.

The Northern Watersnake can get quite large and heavy bodied. The scales are keeled. They can be gray, tan or brown with dark brown or reddish brown bands on the front of its body. Farther back the bands break up and become disconnected. The pattern is most vivid on juveniles and younger snakes (though note colorful adult in main photo). Older, larger snakes often have little visible pattern, especially if dry. The belly is white with red or brown half moons (inset photo).

Courtship, Mating & Young: Northern Watersnakes mate on land or in the water. Females give birth to 4 to 99 live young, most often 15 to 40. It takes two or three years before the young reach maturity.

A rare photo of a wild Northern Watersnake hunting fish or frogs in a fastwater stream.

Diet: Cold-blooded vertebrates such as fish, frogs, tadpoles and salamanders.

Nature Notes:

Northern Watersnakes have nasty dispositions and will bite viciously. Some people mistake them for the cotton-mouth, but they don't occur anywhere near the North Woods.

A juvenile watersnake eats a minnow. Fish is a food staple.

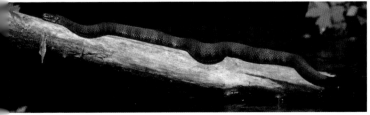

A large, heavy-bodied Northern Watersnake basks in the quiet backwater or a river.

Queen Snake *Regina septemvittata*

| APRIL | MAY | JUNE | JULY | AUG | SEPT | OCT |

Small creeks or streams with rock bottoms and sunlit places for basking.

Nature Notes:

Queen Snakes are fussy eaters. They consume mostly crayfish that have recently shed the hard exoskeleton. After shedding, a crayfish will hide until its new exoskeleton hardens, but the Queen Snake searches them out with its forked tongue and Jacobson's Organ.

Meet the Queen Snake

Description: Length is 15 to 24 inches. Record length of 36¼ inches.

The Queen Snake's scales are keeled. They can be brown, gray or olive with a yellowish stripe along the lower side. Three black stripes, one dorsal and one on each side, are sometimes visible. The belly is yellow with four brown stripes. Juveniles are miniature versions of the adults.

Range Notes: In the North Woods, the Queen Snake occurs only as an isolated population on Bois Blanc Island, which is on the western end of Lake Huron.

Courtship, Mating & Young: Queen Snakes mate in the spring, but may have mated in the fall as well. The female bears 5 to 31 young in late summer. Females probably breed in their third year.

Diet: Crayfish that have recently shed its hard exoskeleton.

Nature Notes:

Queen Snakes are more secretive than water snakes. They bask, but are quick to dive into the water if disturbed. They often hide under submerged rocks.

Butler's Gartersnake *Thamnophis butleri*

| APRIL | MAY | JUNE | JULY | AUG | SEPT | OCT |

Grassy areas adjacent to marshes and other wetlands, prairies, fields and vacant lots.

Nature Notes:

Darting away into grass or brush is the normal gartersnake escape strategy. Butler's Gartersnake is no exception unless protective cover is too distant. The snake then whips its head back and forth while looping its body from side to side. The exaggerated motion may somehow confuse a predator.

Meet the Butler's Gartersnake

Description: Length is 15 to 20 inches. Record length of 27¼ inches.

Butler's Gartersnake has keeled scales and a small head, only slightly larger than the neck. There are three yellow or orange stripes, one dorsal and one on each side. The side stripe is located on scale row 3 ↑ and adjacent halves of rows 2 and 4 (on anterior of body). The ground color is brown, black or olive and sometimes contains two rows of black spots. The belly is greenish and edged with brown. Juveniles are similarly colored.

Courtship, Mating & Young: Butler's Gartersnakes breed after emerging from hibernation. Many snakes may be at the site and breeding can be very competitive. Receptive females are identified by scent and one or sev-

Note that the Butler's Gartersnake has a small head compared to the body.

eral males will attempt copulation. A successful male leaves a mucus-like plug in the
female's cloaca, which prevents other males
from breeding with her for several days.
Females give birth to 4 to 20 young, usually in
late July or August.

Diet: Feeds mostly on earthworms, but small
amphibians are also prey.

Nature Notes:

Butler's Gartersnake
feeds mostly on earth-
worms, but small
amphibians are also
prey items.

The side stripe is on scale row 3
and parts of rows 2 and 4.

Common Gartersnake *Thamnophis sirtalis*

| APRIL | MAY | JUNE | JULY | AUG | SEPT | OCT |

Almost any habitat that is in the vicinity of water, including forests, prairies, meadows, marshes, suburbs and vacant lots.

Nature Notes:

Gartersnakes are quick to escape into tall grass or brush if danger threatens. Sometimes they coil and spread out the body to look bigger. Like many other snakes, when grabbed, they bite and release a foul smelling musk from glands at the base of the tail. Neither defense is more than mildly annoying, but it often works.

Meet the Common Gartersnake

Description: Length is 18 to 26 inches. Record length for the eastern subspecies is 48¼ inches.

The scales are keeled. Three yellow stripes are usually prominent against a background of black, brown or olive. The side stripes are located on scale rows 2 and 3 ↑.

Many Common Gartersnakes look spotted or checkered, having two rows of alternating black spots between the dorsal and lateral stripes. The belly can be yellow, pale green, pale blue, tan or cream color. Juveniles are miniature versions of the adults.

Courtship, Mating & Young: Large numbers of Common Gartersnakes often hibernate together and are ready to breed when they emerge. The result is intense competition to reproduce and a couple dirty tricks to increase

A Green Frog becomes lunch for this gartersnake.

chances of success. Several males may be simultaneously attempting to mate with a single female, creating a ball of squirming snakes. Some males secrete an odor mimicking a female, which might increase their chances by distracting other males. Sometimes a male, having successfully copulated with a female, will leave a plug of mucus-like substance inside her cloaca that insures no other males can breed with her for several days.

In August or early September, anywhere from 3 to 80 (more likely 10 to 40) young are born. They can join the breeding ball in their second or third year.

Diet: Feed mostly on cold-blooded prey such as frogs, toads, salamanders, fish and worms.

Gartersnakes will take fish from small wetlands.

Eastern Ribbonsnake *Thamnophis sauritus*

| APRIL | MAY | JUNE | JULY | AUG | SEPT | OCT |

Sphagnum bogs and the edges of streams and marshes where there is plenty of low vegetation.

Meet the Eastern Ribbonsnake

Nature Notes:

Eastern Ribbonsnakes cruise the surface of shallow water and move through shoreline vegetation as they hunt small salamanders, salamander larvae, frogs and tadpoles. They often climb into bushes to bask in the sun.

Description: Length is 18 to 26 inches.

The Eastern Ribbonsnake is a slim garter-snake. The head and eyes are large ↑ and the labials are white with no dark edges. The scales are keeled. The tail is long, being between one fourth and one third of the total length. The three stripes may be yellow, greenish yellow or white, but the middle stripe could be brown. The lateral stripe is on scale rows 3 and 4 with a brown stripe below. The belly is pale green, yellowish or white. Juveniles have the same coloration as adults.

Courtship, Mating & Young: Eastern Ribbonsnakes breed after emerging from hibernation, and in late July or August the female crawls to somewhat higher ground to bear her 3 to 26 young. They will be adults in their second or third year.

Diet: Small salamanders, frogs and tadpoles.

Nature Notes:

Hibernation can be in low places, such as crayfish burrows or in sites on higher ground with other snakes.

Massasauga *Sistrurus catenatus*

APRIL	MAY	JUNE	JULY	AUG	SEPT	OCT

River bottom forests, swamps and wet prairies. They often move to nearby fields in the summer.

Meet the Massasauga

Nature Notes:

Heat-sensing pits help detect and locate warm-blooded prey. The snake strikes and the hollow fangs inject venom. Injury is avoided by waiting for the venom to act. Then it uses its tongue and Jacobson's organ to track its meal.

Massasaugas hibernate individually in crayfish burrows or other burrows, and they emerge with spring flooding.

Description: Length is 20 to 32 inches.

The Massasauga is heavy-bodied with a small rattle ↑. The head is large, widened at the rear and clearly larger than the neck. There is a pit between the eye and nostril. The eye has a vertical pupil and there is a broad dark line from the eye to the neck. The scales are keeled. The body is gray, brown or dark brown with darker blotches. Sometimes the blotches are edged with white. The blotches turn to bands on the tail. The belly is mostly black. Juveniles are similarly colored, but the rattle is only a single prebutton on newborn snakes.

Courtship, Mating & Young: Massasaugas breed in fall and spring, although many females only breed every other year. The 5 to 20 young are born in August or early

Five to twenty young are born live in August or early September.

September. The newborn Massasaugas are capable of using their fangs and venom. They become sexually mature in their third or fourth year.

Diet: Voles and deer mice primarily, but also frogs, snakes, birds and bird eggs.

Nature Notes:

The Massasauga is not an aggressive snake and uses its protective camouflage to avoid being bothered. When threatened, it will coil and vibrate its tail, although its rattle is not very loud, resembling the buzz of an insect.

Notice the facial pit and vertical pupil; traits of rattlesnakes.

This juvenile Massasauga only has a pre-button for a rattle.

Glossary

Aberrant: Coloration different than normal for the species.

Adhesive disc: Enlarged toe tip of a frog in the treefrog family.

Aestivation: A state of dormancy during prolonged heat or drought. Also estivation.

Amplexus: The sexual embrace of male and female frog or toad.

Anal plate: The enlarged scale (single or divided) in front of, or covering a snake's vent.

Annuli: Concentric annual growth rings evident on the scutes of some turtles.

Anterior: Towards the front.

Anuran: A frog or toad.

AOR: "Alive on road" when recording data on an amphibian or reptile.

Arboreal: Living in trees.

Arthropod: An animal with jointed legs but no backbone, such as insects or spiders.

Autotomy: Loss of the tail as a defensive adaptation.

Barbel: A small fleshy skin projection on the chin or neck of a turtle.

Bask: Warming in the sun.

Beak: The sharp sheath covering turtle jaws and a tadpole's horny mouthparts.

Boss: A large bump between the eyes of some toads.

Bridge: The part of a turtle's shell connecting the carapace and plastron.

Brille: The clear scale covering the eye of a snake.

Carapace: The upper part of a turtle's shell.

Carnivorous: Eating animals, not plants.

Carrion: Dead animals.

Caruncle: Temporary, sharp tooth-like structure on the snout of a hatchling turtle.

Caudal: Referring to the tail.

Cirri: A pair of tiny points projecting downward from upper lip of some salamanders.

Clutch: The eggs deposited at one time by one female.

Cloaca: The internal chamber that temporarily holds wastes or reproductive materials.

Colony: A small, isolated local population of an animal species.

Costal: Referring to the rib area.

Costal grooves: Vertical grooves on the sides of salamanders.

Cranial: Referring to the skull.

Crepuscular: Most active at dawn or dusk.

Crests: Ridge-like structures on top of the head of some toads.

Crustacean: Aquatic arthropods with hard shells, such as a crayfish.

Cryptic: Camouflage coloration.

Cusp: A pointed tooth-like projection.

Dermal: Referring to the skin.

Diploid: Body cell containing two sets of chromosomes; one from each parent.

Disjunct: A population geographically separated from the main range of a species.

Diurnal: Active during daylight.

DOR: "Dead on road" when recording data on an amphibian or reptile.

Dorsal: Referring to the back.

Dorsolateral: Referring to the area along the upper side.

Dorsolateral fold: A raised ridge along the upper sides of some frogs.

Dorsolateral ridge: A raised ridge along the upper sides of some frogs.

Dorsum: The upper surface.

Ecdysis: The shedding of the skin.

Ectotherm: An animal that gains its body heat from the environment.

Eft: Terrestrial stage of the newt.

Egg tooth: A temporary tooth used by snakes and lizards to slice the egg shell.

Endotherm: An animal that generates its own heat by metabolism.

Ephemeral: Temporary.

Estivation: A state of dormancy during prolonged heat or drought. Also aestivation.

Extirpated: All individuals of a species are removed or destroyed in a specific region.

Facial pit: The heat-sensitive organ located between the eye and nostril of pit vipers.

Femoral: Refers to the thigh.

Fossorial: Living underground.

Gelatinous: Jelly-like.

Genus: A taxonomic group between family and species, containing one or more species.

Globular: Rounded like a ball.

Gravid: Pregnant.

Gular: Referring to the throat.

Hemipenes: The paired copulatory organs of male lizards and snakes.

Herbivorous: Eating plants, not animals.

Herp: An amphibian or reptile.

Herpetofauna: The amphibians and reptiles of a specific area.

Herpetology: The study of amphibians and reptiles.

Hibernaculum: The den or place an animal spends the winter.

Hinge: The joint between two movable sections of plastron in some turtles.

Hybrid: The offspring of two different species.

Intergrade: The offspring of two different subspecies.

Invertebrate: Any animal with no backbone.

Keel: A raised ridge.

Keratin: A tough protein composing the outer covering of reptile skin and scales.

Labial: Referring to the lip area.

Lamina: Scute or plate of a turtle shell.

Larva: Immature aquatic form of some amphibians.

Lateral: Refers to the side of the body.

Lateral line: A series of sensory receptors along the upper side of the body.

Marginal scutes: The small scutes along the outer edge of a turtle's carapace.

Medial: Refers to the middle or midline.

Melanin: Dark pigment granules found in skin cells.

Melanistic: An animal that is abnormally dark or black.

Mental gland: A gland under the chin of some male salamanders.

Metamorphosis: The change in body form from aquatic to land stage.

Middorsal: Referring to the middle of the back.

Mimicry: One species resembling another to increase survival chances.

Mollusk: Group of invertebrates including snails, slugs and clams.

Morphology: The appearance, form or structure of an animal.

Nape: The back of the neck.

Nasolabial groove: A tiny groove extending from nostril to mouth of some salamanders.

Neotenic: Describes a salamander that retains larval features as an adult.

Neoteny: Larval reproduction because metamorphosis is delayed.

Niche: An animal's place in an ecosystem, especially in the food chain.

Nictitating membrane: A transparent third eyelid that protects the eye underwater.

Nuchal: Referring to the neck area.

Ocelli: Dark or light edged circular spots.

Omnivorous: Eating both animal and plant material.

Oviparous: Egg-laying.

Ovoviviparous: Young develop in the body, but nurtured by yolk sac not placenta.

Papillae: Small fleshy projections around a tadpole's mouth.

Parotoid glands: A pair of large poison glands behind a toad's eyes.

Pectoral: Referring to the chest area.

Pheromone: A chemical used as a signal to an animal of the same species.

Plastron: The bottom part of a turtle's shell.

Plates: Large reptile scales, especially on a turtle shell.

Poikilothermic: An animal with no internal control of its body temperature.

Posterior: Toward the rear of an animal.

Postocular: Behind the eye.

Progenic: When the larval form of some salamanders are able to reproduce.

Radio telemetry: Tracking an animal's movements by attaching a tiny radio transmitter.

Regenerate: To re-grow a lost body part, such as a lizard tail.

Release call: A call given by a male anuran when clasped by another male.

Relict population: A remaining group of a species, left isolated by a shrinking range.

Reticulate: A netlike pattern of linear markings.

Rostral: Scale on the tip of the snout.

Rostrum: Snout or nose.

Scale: An outgrowth of keratin from reptile skin

Scute: A large scale, such as on a turtle shell or a snake's belly.

Septal: Referring to a partition or wall.

Serrate: Saw-toothed.

Sexual dimorphism: Difference in form between the sexes.

Smooth scales: Reptile scales with no keel.

Snout-vent length: Length of an amphibian or reptile not including the tail.

Species: Group of similar organisms that can interbreed.

Spectacle: The clear scale covering a snake's eye.

Spermatheca: A cloacal gland or tubules that store sperm in a female salamander.

Spermatophore: A gelatinous mass capped by sperm deposited by a male salamander to be picked up by the female.

Spiracle: A short tube that discharges water from a tadpole's gill chamber.

Sympatric: Occupying the same geographic area.

Tadpole: The aquatic larval stage of a frog or tadpole.

Taxon: A group of organisms in a classification system.

Terminal: At the end or tip.

Terrestrial: living on land.

Tetraploid: An animal with double the normal number of chromosomes.

Tetrapod: An animal with four limbs or descended from one. Amphibians, reptiles, birds and mammals are tetrapods.

Thermoregulation: Controlling body temperature by behavior.

Tibia: The leg between the knee and ankle. Also, a lower leg bone.

Transverse: Perpendicular to the long axis of the body or body part.

Tubercle: A small rounded skin projection.

Tympanum: External eardrum of most anurans and turtles.

Vent: The external opening of the cloaca.

Ventral: Refers to the belly.

Ventrals: The wide belly scales of snakes.

Vertebral: The middle of the back.

Viviparous: Bearing live young that were nourished through a placenta.

Appendix A
Checklist of North Woods Herps

SALAMANDERS Order Caudata
- ❏ Mudpuppy   *Necturus maculosus*
- ❏ Central Newt   *Notophthalmus viridescens louisianensis*
- ❏ Red-spotted Newt   *Notophthalmus viridescens viridescens*
- ❏ Blue-spotted Salamander   *Ambystoma laterale*
- ❏ Spotted Salamander   *Ambystoma maculatum*
- ❏ Tiger Salamander   *Ambystoma tigrinum*
- ❏ Four-toed Salamander   *Hemidactylium scutatum*
- ❏ Eastern Red-backed Salamander   *Plethodon cinereus*

FROGS & TOADS Order Anura
- ❏ American Toad   *Bufo americanus*
- ❏ Fowler's Toad   *Bufo fowleri*
- ❏ Canadian Toad   *Bufo hemiophrys*
- ❏ Cope's Gray Treefrog   *Hyla chrysoscelis*
- ❏ Gray Treefrog   *Hyla versicolor*
- ❏ Spring Peeper   *Pseudacris crucifer*
- ❏ Boreal Chorus Frog   *Pseudacris maculata*
- ❏ Western Chorus Frog   *Pseudacris triseriata*
- ❏ American Bullfrog   *Rana catesbeiana*
- ❏ Green Frog   *Rana clamitans*
- ❏ Pickerel Frog   *Rana palustris*
- ❏ Northern Leopard Frog   *Rana pipiens*
- ❏ Mink Frog   *Rana septentrionalis*
- ❏ Wood Frog   *Rana sylvatica*

TURTLES Order Testudines
- ❏ Snapping Turtle   *Chelydra serpentina*
- ❏ Stinkpot   *Sternotherus odoratus*
- ❏ Western Painted Turtle   *Chrysemys picta bellii*
- ❏ Midland Painted Turtle   *Chrysemys picta marginata*
- ❏ Spotted Turtle   *Clemmys guttata*
- ❏ Blanding's Turtle   *Emydoidea blandingii*
- ❏ Wood Turtle   *Glyptemys insculpta*
- ❏ Northern Map Turtle   *Graptemys geographica*
- ❏ Eastern Box Turtle   *Terrapene carolina*
- ❏ Spiny Softshell   *Apalone spinifera*

LIZARDS & SNAKES Order Squamata
- ❏ Common Five-lined Skink   *Eumeces fasciatus*
- ❏ Prairie Skink   *Eumeces septentrionalis*
- ❏ Eastern Racer   *Coluber constrictor*
- ❏ Western Foxsnake   *Elaphe vulpina*
- ❏ Milksnake   *Lampropeltis triangulum*
- ❏ Smooth Greensnake   *Opheodrys vernalis*
- ❏ Ring-necked Snake   *Diadophis punctatus*
- ❏ Eastern Hog-nosed Snake   *Heterodon platirhinos*
- ❏ DeKay's Brownsnake   *Storeria dekayi*
- ❏ Red-bellied Snake   *Storeria occipitomaculata*
- ❏ Northern Watersnake   *Nerodia sipedon*
- ❏ Queen Snake   *Regina septemvittata*
- ❏ Butler's Gartersnake   *Thamnophis butleri*
- ❏ Common Gartersnake   *Thamnophis sirtalis*
- ❏ Eastern Ribbonsnake   *Thamnophis sauritus*
- ❏ Massasauga   *Sistrurus catenatus*

Appendix B
Titles of Interest

Christoffel, R., R. Hay, and M. Monroe. 2002. *Turtles and Lizards of Wisconsin*. Madison, WI: Wisconsin Department of Natural Resources.

Christoffel, R., R. Hay, and L. Ramirez. 2000. *Snakes of Wisconsin*. Madison, WI: Wisconsin Department of Natural Resources.

Christoffel, R., R. Hay, and M. Wolfgram. 2001. *Amphibians of Wisconsin*. Madison, WI: Department of Natural Resources.

Conant, R., and J. T. Collins. 1998. *A Field Guide to Reptiles and Amphibians of Eastern and Central North America*. 3rd ed. Boston, MA: Houghton Mifflin Co.

Harding, J. H. 1997. *Amphibians and Reptiles of the Great Lakes Region*. Ann Arbor, MI: University of Michigan Press.

Harding, J. H., and J. A. Holman. 1992. *Michigan Frogs, Toads, and Salamanders*. East Lansing, MI: Michigan State University Museum.

Harding, J. H., and J. A. Holman. 1990. *Michigan Turtles and Lizards*. East Lansing, MI: Michigan State University Museum.

Holman, J. A., J. H. Harding, M. M. Hensley, and G. R. Dudderar. 1989. East Lansing: Michigan State University Museum.

Karns, D. R. 1986. *Field Herpetology: Methods for the Study of Amphibians and Reptiles in Minnesota*. Minneapolis, MN: Bell Museum of Natural History

Moriarty, J. J. 2004. *Turtles and Turtle Watching for the North Central States*. St. Paul, MN: Minnesota Department of Natural Resources.

Oldfield, B., and J. J. Moriarty. 1994. *Amphibians and Reptiles Native to Minnesota*. Minneapolis, MN: University of Minnesota Press.

Shaw, J. 1987. *John Shaw's Closeups in Nature*. New York, NY: Amphoto.

Trauth, S. E., H. W. Robison, and M. V. Plummer. *The Amphibians and Reptiles of Arkansas*. 2004. Fayetteville, AR: University of Arkansas Press.

Tyning, T. F. 1990. *Stokes Nature Guides: A Guide to Amphibians and Reptiles*. Boston, MA: Little, Brown.

Vogt, R. C. 1981. *Natural History of Amphibians and Reptiles of Wisconsin*. Milwaukee, WI: Milwaukee Public Museum.

West, L., and W. P. Leonard. 1997. *How to Photograph Reptiles and Amphibians*. Mechanicsburg, PA: Stackpole Books.

Appendix C
Additional References

Blasus, R. F. 1997. *Amphibian & Reptile Time Table For Minnesota.* Minneapolis, MN: Minnesota Herpetological Society Occasional Paper 4.

Parmelee, J. R., M. G. Knutson, and J. E. Lyon. 2002. *A Field Guide to Amphibian Larvae and Eggs of Minnesota, Wisconsin and Iowa.* Washington D.C.: U. S. Geological Survey.

Sheldon, A. B. 2005. *Northern Water Snake.* Big River Magazine. Sept.: 28-31.

Sheldon, A. B. 2004. *Wading for a Photo Op: Secrets of Shooting Frogs at Night.* Big River Magazine. March: 18-19, 25-27.

Sheldon, A. B. 1997. *Night Photography: Frogs & Toads.* Reptile & Amphibian Magazine. March: 70-73.

Sheldon, A. B. 1995. *Photographing Wild Reptiles.* Reptile & Amphibian Magazine. July: 76-83.

Watermolen, D. J. 1995. *A Key to the Eggs of Wisconsin's Amphibians.* Madison, WI: Wisconsin Department of Natural Resources.

Frog & Toad Calls

Elliot, L. 1992. *The Calls of Frogs and Toads: Eastern and Central North America.* Post Mills, VT: Chelsea Green Publishing.

Kellogg, P. P., A. A. Allen, and T. Wiewandt, 1982 *Voices of the Night: The Calls of the Frogs and Toads of Eastern North America.*

Resources

B&H Photo, 800-947-6628, www.bhphotovideo.com
Camera equipment.

Kirk Enterprises, 800-626-5074, www.kirkphoto.com
Tripods, quick release plates.

Midwest Tongs, 877-US-TONGS, www.tongs.com
Snake hooks and tongs.

Reptiles magazine, 949-855-8822
Monthly magazine on amphibians and reptiles.

The Slideprinter, 303-698-2962
Prints, duplicate slides.

Zoo Book Sales, 507-467-8733, www.zoobooksales.com
Amphibian and reptiles books.

Index

Photo Credits

Allen Blake Sheldon: All photos are by the author except those noted below.

Photos are numbered from top left of the page clockwise (e.g. "a" is top left).

Anne Elliot: 64, 65

James Gerholdt: 56, 57

Jim Harding: 128, 134

Dan Nedrelo: 53b

Beth Sheldon: 17

Sparky Stensaas (www.stoneridgepress.com): 11a, 53d, 82, 83f, 95a.

Field Notes

Field Notes

Field Notes

Other user-friendly field guides from Kollath+Stensaas Publishing

Dragonflies
of the
North Woods

ISBN
0-9673793-6-9

Damselflies
of the
North Woods

ISBN
0-9673793-7-7

Spiders
of the
North Woods

ISBN
0-9673793-4-2

Butterflies
of the
North Woods

ISBN
0-9673793-8-5